COUNT ON READING

Tips for Planning Reading Motivation Programs

Compiled and edited by Susan D. Ballard

American Association of School Librarians
A division of the American Library Association

Published by the American Association of School Librarians, a division of the American Library Association

This publication can be purchased from the American Library Association, 50 East Huron Street, Chicago, Illinois 60611

Cover and text design and layout by NeigerDesignInc., in Futura and Novarese on a Power Macintosh 7500/100 using Quark Express software supported by Adobe Illustrator and Adobe Photoshop. Cover printed on 26" Komori in three colors. Interior pages printed on 40" Heidelberg 2 color perfector in one color.

Cover printed on 80# Cougar Opaque cover. Interior pages printed on 84 pages of 80# Cougar Opaque text. Printed and perfect bound by hc Johnson Press, 2801 Eastrock Drive, Rockford, IL 61109.

The paper used in this publication meets the minimum requirements of the American National Standards for Information Sciences — Permanence of Paper for Printed Library Materials, ANSI Z39.48 1992 ∞.

ISBN 0-8389-7892-4

Printed in the United States of America.

Table of Contents

David V. Loertscher

ount on Reading was born at an American Library Association (ALA) Midwinter Meeting when Henry Cisneros, the key-note speaker, begged the association to do something about the growing gap in our society between the haves and the have nots. But what can libraries really do? I had become acquainted with the work of Stephen Krashen just before the meeting and knew that one of the major keys to literacy was access to lots of reading material and lots of practice. It was apparent that libraries had always been a quiet, but major contributor to the nation's literacy quotient. Too quiet.

So many people in this nation take libraries for granted. It's a case of benevolent neglect. Are libraries a key to national literacy? That could be a nice slogan, but there are, you know, so many other pressing problems. Besides, many private and corporate interests and groups were already sponsoring reading initiatives at the time. Weren't there enough already? How could one more initiative succeed in an ocean of options?

As hundreds of ideas were given from many interested persons, the notion came that Count on Reading need not act to replace a single good program in any community, state, or nation. Rather, it would seek to join hands with any or all efforts and would serve as the "report card" for those efforts. So whether you were into Book It!, Accelerated Reader, National Library Week, National Children's Book Week, Summer Reading Clubs, MS Readathons — it did not matter. We could link all of them in such a way that the total effort would last long enough to help children and young people acquire the reading habit.

So, Count on Reading counts. It doesn't matter who participates, or whether tallies are exact, or who ends up getting the credit — the emphasis is on joining together to get a job done over a long period of time. And the emphasis is always upon the individual young person. Every reader gaining the reading habit is one more to add to the pot. One more added to the opportunity column. One more child who can understand what the American Dream is and has the ability to learn how to achieve it.

Count on Reading was never set up as a contest. It is a challenge! Every reader who could read just one more book was to help the nation achieve its goal. As you will see by reading the articles here, every state and community responded differently with different rules, techniques, ideas, strategies, etc. But the wonder of it is that success was home grown. It is a model that governments might examine for its richness in civic improvement.

Hundreds and hundreds of people have given time, energy, money, and encouragement to the project. None of us knows the real measure of the goodness of the project - but we can all be certain that every avid reader born during the project has better comprehension, spelling, grammar, vocabulary, and writing style.

And yet, with all we have done and are doing, the need for basic literacy is a constant problem. It doesn't go away. Every year there are a new crop of avid readers, struggling read-ers, and nonreaders. Efforts in your community — your home, your neighborhood — cannot stop. The advent of information technology requires that every person must know how to read and read critically.

Please use the articles and ideas here. They contain a great deal of wisdom on how to bring communities together in a common cause. Learn to spread that effort over a long period of time, inviting new partners, adapting to fresh ideas, but keep the same focus on the fact that if you want a literate community **IT'S AMOUNT THAT COUNTS**.

continued on next page

In closing, I would would like to share a few dreams:

1. I wish that every school and public library would add at least one new fresh and exciting title for every young person they serve — one book a kid a year. How can we attract young people to outdated, dilapidated, unattractive book collections and expect them to want to read? Our major Internet suppliers want just $20 a month for unlimited usages. I wish we spent $20 a month on every young person for books they'd like to read.

2. I wish every kid in this nation could check out an unlimited supply of books from the school and the public library. They can't. In too many places youngsters can't even check out any books and when they are allowed, they get one or two books a week. It is a crime — a national disgrace. We cannot build a literate nation with these kinds of rules. If your community schools and libraries have solved this problem, then every child benefits.

3. I wish every kindergartner and first grader were carrying home two different books every night from school — one to be read to them and one to "read" by themselves. It would be a start.

4. I wish every young person had a public library card and used it.

5. I wish a major funder would come forward so that Count on Reading could continue to reach toward the billion-book goal and beyond.

And finally,

6. I wish there were more and better books for children from every diverse culture and heritage. There are still areas where there are just a very few

really good titles. My own life has been enriched as I have ached with others who have suffered prejudice, laughed and cried across the cultures and time periods, and discovered that I wasn't the only one trying to solve life's challenges. I have been prepared well for the information society. Can we deny the next generation the same opportunity?

David V. Loertscher, is a past president of the American Association of School Librarians. Count on Reading was one of his presidential initiatives. Loertscher is currently a professor for the School of Library and Information Science at San Jose State University in San Jose, California.

Acknowledgements

Susan D. Ballard

Alot of people have contributed a lot of time and talent to make this publication possible. It began with **David Loertscher's** dream to ensure that America's children have access to print-rich environments so thick with good things to read that they are lured into the habit of reading and maintain it throughout their lives. No dream can be more crucial to achieve, or find a better visionary than David to strive for it's fulfillment.

David's dream was shared by his great friend and colleague, **Blanche Woolls**, who helped to guide Count on Reading, as a national initiative, through the sometimes turbulent waters of organizational culture. No cause ever had so true a champion.

Brenda White, first national chair of the initiative, and her successor, the current chair, **Bettie Estes-Rickner**, provided the necessary leadership to nurture and then guide Count on Reading to reach full potential. No endeavor ever had such sterling direction.

Count on Reading Committee members have demonstrated, through hours of work and effort, that theirs was a project of purpose, and they were proud to commit to it's realization. Special appreciation is extended to two members - **Marjorie Horowitz**, who recruited and welcomed state coordinators with panache, and our own "Count" **Don DeWeese**, who delights all when he announces the tally. No committee ever had such *espirit de corps*.

The wonderful folks at **Follett Software Company** know a good thing when they see it, and they have provided generous support to the Count on Reading effort in order to make promotional materials widely available. Follett recognizes that there is a strong connection between reading and the ability to use rapidly-advancing information technologies, and they have been generous in providing funding and encouraging their personnel to work in partnership with the American Association of School Librarians (AASL). No benefactor could have been better company.

This enterprise has also been the beneficiary of lots of tender loving care from the AASL Staff. **Lisa Wolfe**, former Coordinator for Communications, helped to conceptualize this manuscript and her editorial ability made sense of it as it neared completion. **Margaret Lewis**, former Program Assistant, and **Josephine Sharif**, Coordinator for Publications, have been of great support in helping me bring this book to a happy conclusion. No staff could have been as caring and professional.

Much of the success enjoyed by the reading initiative can be tied back to the review of research provided by **Stephen Krashen** in his book *The Power of Reading*. AASL is happy to point out the connections between many of the remarkable efforts of our members and Krashen's work. No work has been as important for those of us involved in reading promotion, as that of Stephen Krashen.

Lastly, I am grateful to the *Count on Reading Handbook* contributors. As you meet **Kimberly Taylor, Susan Snider, Shelly Senator, Anne Masters** and **Linda Cornwell**, you will be struck by the relaxed and conversational tone with which they tell their stories. I know that as I worked with their materials I was, more often than not, figuring out how I would adopt, adapt, and modify all of the wonderful ideas and strategies they provided. Their chronicles of success illustrate the reason to continue to make every effort to proceed with the development and implementation of reading initiatives based on solid research. No accounts could be more compelling.

Introduction

Susan D. Ballard

*T*he Count on Reading Handbook *is geared to school library media specialists, children's librarians and educators interested in developing a reading motivation program. It provides information about how and why to develop a successful program in a school, state or region.*

Count on Reading, a national reading initiative sponsored by the American Association of School Librarians, was designed to challenge the nation's young people to read a billion books, and to become avid readers. By linking reading initiatives throughout the country, Count on Reading helped to demonstrate and document the long-term impact of avid reading and to leverage the efforts of millions of youngsters, and the people who guide their reading habits. One billion books is a milestone not to be taken lightly! One billion half-inch books equals the diameter of the earth!

And yet, there were more compelling reasons to encourage and motivate youth to participate in this endeavor. Research shows that students must read a lot to become good readers, and research also confirms that good readers are superior in reading comprehension, spelling, writing style, vocabulary and grammar. This is the essence of the work of Stephen Krashen in his book *The Power of Reading* — a review of more than 100 years of reading research. Krashen, in his analysis of the evidence, clearly underscores the importance of free, voluntary reading in helping to create readers. Independent reading is key. The 1985 report of the National Commission on Reading, Becoming a Nation of Readers, also recognized that "independent reading is probably a major source of reading fluency. In contrast to workbook pages or computer drills, the reading of books provides practice in the whole act of reading. Practice in this form is likely to be particularly effective in increasing the automaticity of word identification skills. Avid readers do twenty times or more as much reading. This means they are getting vastly more practice and helps explain why children who read a lot make more progress in reading." And so how do Krashen, the National Commission on Reading and others suggest that we create readers? They tell us where readers come from and to what techniques they respond.

Becoming a Nation of Readers reminds us that "children who are avid readers come from homes in which reading is encouraged by a parent, grandparent, older brother or sister, or even a baby sitter. They come from homes that have books, subscriptions to children's magazines, and in which both adults and children have library cards." The importance of good reading models cannot be overstated.

Krashen's research also emphasizes that models help and reviews the techniques which are most likely to produce long-term results and keep kids reading. Other factors identified as having lasting value include:

- Create a print-rich environment at home, in the classroom, and in the library.

- Provide unlimited access to materials from libraries.

- Allow young people to read what they like to read — including light reading and comics.

- Read aloud to young people everyday — K–12!

- Use sustained silent reading as a tool.

- Encourage reading — but intrinsic rewards may not be the best technique.

As you read about a variety of successful state Count on Reading initiatives, existing programs that linked to the effort, and about the kind of activities designed to develop readers, you will find that putting the research to the test was exactly the exercise needed in order to produce desired results. Time and time again, kids responded to initiatives where elements of an effective independent reading program were in place. Watch for those themes

continued on next page

in the efforts of Colorado, New Hampshire, Connecticut, and Oklahoma to develop their programs and the strategies employed in Indiana school settings by participants in Project REAP. In fact, Indiana's Project REAP, an endeavor of the Department of Education's Center for School Improvement and Performance funded by the Lilly Endowment, Inc., provides a checklist for the very elements we need to strive to put in place. Readers are nurtured in schools where:

- Teachers recognize the value of independent reading.

- Students have access to a wide variety of reading materials.

- Students are provided time within the school day to read material of their own choosing.

- Students are read to every day.

- Students engage in a wide variety of activities related to reading.

- Students are provided with opportunities to respond to reading with others.

Count on Reading will not end with the realization of one billion books. The lesson it aspires to instill — the love of reading for its own sake — will continue to need to be nurtured by teachers, librarians, parents and all concerned with providing the next generation with the essential skill for success. We've all heard the old story about a person needing directions, who stops to ask a passer-by "How do you get to Carnegie Hall?"; only to be told, "Practice, practice, practice." How do our youth achieve their goals and aspirations? Reading, reading, and more reading! You can count on it.

PART ONE

SUCCESSFUL COUNT ON READING PROGRAMS

Read the Rockies, Colorado Style

Kimberly Taylor

Coloradans read more than three million books in a six-month period in 1995, as part of a challenge called "Read the Rockies." Using the national Count on Reading campaign as a springboard, this tailor-made-for-Colorado promotion included diverse segments of the community such as schools, businesses and even prisons.

Initial Organization and Partner Strengths

In January 1995, a group of people gathered to brainstorm Colorado's participation in the national "Count on Reading" program. The initial committee consisted of people from the Aurora Public Library, Colorado Center for the Book, Colorado State Library, Denver Public Schools, *Rocky Mountain News* and the Tattered Cover Bookstore. Each committee member was selected based on their reputation as "workers" and/or ability to make a contribution in a broader sense. Lynda Welborn, then with the State Library, organized the meeting. Lynda brought contacts and resources of the State Library to the table. Libraries Unlimited, a publisher, donated the logo design for the campaign. The Colorado Center for the Book coordinates the statewide National Library Week (NLW) promotion and agreed to use "Read the Rockies" as the theme for NLW in 1995. The *Rocky Mountain News* committed to run a monthly tally through their mini-pages. Representatives of the Aurora Public Library, Denver Public Schools and the Tattered Cover Bookstore had promotional expertise and the resources of their patrons to lend to the effort. Later, the Colorado Department of Education joined and contributed $1,000 to get the word out to a variety of their constituents.

Creating a Theme and Making It Work for You

Several things worked together to make this program a success. First, the name "Read the Rockies" is a word play on a very popular sporting event in Colorado called "Ride the Rockies." People enjoyed the new twist. Three million was chosen as a goal because it seemed attainable and that is roughly the population of Colorado. A theme hadn't been chosen for National Library Week. The Colorado Center for the Book (CCFTB) had a budget of $2,000 to create promotional packets for libraries that they could use for National Library Week. By making the National Library Week theme "Read the Rockies," there was suddenly a budget and a staff to manage and promote the first phase of the project.

Project Time Frame

The Colorado Center for the Book also had promoted an event the previous year called "Take Ten." The idea involved asking partici-pants, wherever they were on October 10 at 10 a.m., to stop what they were doing and read. The decision was made that "Take Ten" would be a good culminating activity for Read the Rockies.

In January and early February, Libraries Unlimited created the logo design. In January the Colorado Center for the Book wrote the promotional packet, and in February, one thousand packets were sent to school, academic, special and public libraries around the state. In April, the *Rocky Mountain News* started their promo-tion, and the Colorado Center for the Book sent press releases around the state. The committee continued to contact businesses and other people who we thought could help get the word out. The Colorado Center for the Book also oversees the statewide summer reading program. All of the materials urged librarians to tally the number of books their summer reading kids read and send them to the committee.

Committee members hosted tally meetings monthly to count the results. By August, the campaign hadn't even reached one million, and there were only six weeks to go. The week of October 10 was stunning. Even though people were asked to send their tallies in monthly, they didn't! The majority of them saw the notice, kept a tally for six months, and sent it all in at once! In a few days, 1.8 million books read were counted.

Reasons for and Indicators of Success

A common theme ran through the correspondence from teach-ers. "Do it again!" People said that the simplicity of the cam-paign made it very easy to participate. The packet listed pages of promotional ideas that organizations could use to get people to tally their scores. The campaign said that people could count anything that can be read toward their goal. People were counting books, newspapers, magazines, and even annual reports. Simple tally sheets that people could photocopy were distributed. A black-and-white copy of a two-sided, easy to reproduce bookmark that could be photocopied and used as a tally marker was also provided to participants. The *Rocky Mountain News* ran a form that could be clipped and used as a tally sheet. There were no rules. There was no verification procedure.

Programs and Activities

The creative ideas people came up with were abundant.

- Kendallvue Elementary School (Morrison, Colorado) reported 8,005 books read, and their goal was to come up with family tallies. The winning families received free books and discounts at the schools fall book fair.

- When Cottonwood Creek Elementary School (Englewood, Colorado) reached its goal of 6,000, the principal climbed up to the roof and read a book to the student body from up on high.

- In Eagle Valley, the elemen-tary school made announce-ments about the number of books read at the end of each day. Their bulletin board showed a "book person" who climbed a mountain and the mile markers indicated the num-ber of books read.

- Students at the Mary Blair Elementary School (Loveland, Colorado) enjoyed three "Reading Under the Stars" nights. Families brought sleeping bags, flashlights and books. They camped out in the gym and tallied their reading productivity for the night.
continued on next page

15

Read the Rockies, Colorado Style

- Skyline Vista Elementary School (Denver, Colorado) made a path around the school that indicated the number of books read. By the end of the promotion their path extended 377.5 feet, representing 10,113 books read.

While the numbers for the program were significantly enhanced by schools, people of all ages participated.

- A seventy-six-year-old couple from Aurora sent their tally in from Tulsa, Oklahoma. They apologized for not submitting higher numbers but explained that their travels had them reading more road maps than books.

- The Delta Correctional Facility added 163 books to the total. The librarian reported that one inmate continued to tally the books he read after he was transferred to another facility that wasn't participating in the program.

- The Colorado Department of Education made a huge thermometer and provided weekly updates on how many books employees had read. They announced it at staff meetings and gave a prize to the employee who read the most books.

Conclusion and Model Checklist

The comment heard most often was "please do this again." This promotion gave people a sense of participating in something important that they were sharing with others all over the state. As a result, the Colorado Center for the Book will do the project again. Here are a few things critical to the success of a campaign like this.

- It must be **school based**. While this is a great promotion and there was broad participation, it was critical to get the school library media specialists involved. It was also important to open it up to the community, giving all book enthusiasts a common goal to work toward.

- It must be **community based**. The name "Read the Rockies" is very much a signature Colorado slogan. People felt that they were part of a Colorado effort and wanted to prove that their community could be counted. The way the materials were written, emphasized local communities feeding into a statewide process. Of course, people relate to the local first, then the statewide and then the national levels.

- **The committee** needs to include people who have organizational resources behind them. This project did not have a big budget tied to it, and it would have been extremely difficult to accomplish without a newspaper sponsor, the resources of the State Library and some of the contributions of the other players. It is also critical that the organization spearheading the effort can stick with it from beginning to end. Early in the process, the committee chair from the State Library announced that she was leaving her position. Had all of the money and resources been from the state library, the project probably would have stopped at that point.

- **A packet** of support materials were critical to the project's success. At first, there was only the National Library Week packet. That was somewhat time specific and geared totally toward libraries. As the phone calls started coming in from the general public, they were told that all they had to do was read, keep some form of tally and send it in. They wanted something concrete. The packet was revised to make it generic enough for anyone who wanted more detail. Having something to send out made people feel like they understood the non-rule rules and then they could participate.

- **The timing** of this campaign was probably not as well thought out as it could have been. The bookends of National Library Week and Take Ten were important. However, those summer months were deadly. Since schools are so critical to success, it seems more logical to work within a school year calendar.

- **The follow-up** with those who participated was pretty weak. The deadline was October 10, and three days later the Colorado Center for the Book was putting on the third annual Rocky Mountain Book Festival. No one was prepared for the tens of thousands of pieces of mail that arrived in one week. A better process for tallying more quickly at the end

and for thanking all of the people who participated needs to be developed next time. A Web page has now been developed, and the next campaign will probably announce that people should check that for the results.

- **Ownership** of this event by the Colorado Center for the Book was critical, but the attitude that permeated this promotion was that it belonged to everyone. All kinds of organizations were encouraged to claim it as their very own and put whatever twist worked for them on it. As an organization, this campaign helped us meet the mission of getting people to read.

- **Simplicity** of concept made so many people participate. As librarians called, they were asked why they thought the enthusiasm for this project was so high. Repeatedly they said because it was a productive "competition" and participation was easy. They could make up the rules, they could tie it into what they already do, they could build it around a time frame that worked for them, and it built a sense of team spirit (i.e. "Yeah, Colorado! We can read three million books!"). Kids who participated truly cared that there was a statewide goal and that by working together, it could be reached.

As an organization, the Colorado Center for the Book exists to keep the message of books and reading in the forefront of the minds of people of all ages. Read the Rockies was an excellent way to sustain interest in books and reading.

Kimberly Taylor is the executive director of the Colorado Center for the Book in Golden, Colorado. She is a member of the Colorado State Count on Reading Committee and state coordinator of "Read the Rockies" campaign.

Read the Rockies, Colorado Style

Read the Rockies

READ THE ROCKIES SAMPLE PARTICIPANTS LETTER

Dear Read the Rockies Participant,

Thank you for your interest in promoting reading in Colorado. A coalition of people interested in reading has gathered together to develop a fun promotion with a serious goal. "Read the Rockies" is designed to encourage residents of Colorado, people of all ages, to contribute to our goal of documenting that three million books were read during a period of six months. The campaign was launched statewide during National Library Week. It will continue through October 14. Enclosed is information on the campaign with suggestions for using it to promote reading

"Read the Rockies" is an umbrella program that places emphasis on developing and keeping the reading habit. The goal is to build a state of readers by encouraging people at all age levels to read. By October 14, we hope to be able to document that Coloradans read three million books in six months. We need your help to do that. By documenting numbers through all of our partnerships we can reach the three million goal. This project is an effort in support of the American Association of School Librarians promotion called "Count on Reading." An effort similar to ours will happen in many states.

The key to the success of this campaign is the community "partners" take it on as their own. Whatever group you are affiliated with, this can become their project that they sponsor in whatever form they choose. We are keeping a running list of our "partners" so please talk to us. We want to know who you are, any anecdotes you have about the promotion, and how many books the people involved with you have read.

Finally, sincere thanks to the core group behind the "Read the Rockies" promotion. They are the Colorado Center for the Book, Colorado State Library and Adult Education Office, Colorado Department of Education, Rocky Mountain New, Tattered Cover, Libraries Unlimited, Denver Public Schools, Aurora Public Library, the Colorado Library Association, and the Colorado Educational Media Association.

Please talk to us! You can reach us by phone (303) 273-5933, by fax (303) 273-5935, by e-mail KEEP9779@aol.com, or by mail at 1301 Arapahoe, Suite 3, Golden, CO 80401. Thank you!

Sincerely,

Kimberly Taylor
Executive Director

As of the press date for the Count on Reading Handbook, the Colorado Center for the Book can be reached by telephone at (303) 839-8320 and by fax at (303) 839-8319.

Program Materials

READ THE ROCKIES PROMOTION EXPLANATION

Read the Rockies is a promotion that was launched on April 9 and will run through October 10. The promotional goal of this campaign is to document that Coloradans can read three million books in six months. The real goal of the campaign is to provide a "hook" for interested parties to encourage the general public to read. We are hoping that communities will get behind the campaign and have fun encouraging their residents to read. Our vision is that whether people are in schools, nursing homes, businesses, book clubs, bookstores, libraries, or restaurants, they will be reading and getting some encouragement to tally their results and turn them in.

Because the intent of this promotion is to encourage people to read, there are no restrictions on what is read. The following equivalences established by the Read the Rockies steering committee are merely suggestions:

Reading Keys

Ten newspaper articles =	1 Book
One newspaper in Education Mini Page =	1 Book
One magazine =	1 Book
Three comic books =	1 Book
Ten newsletters =	1 Book

If you would like something to be included that is not listed here, establish a reasonable equivalency, include it in your tally, and send it in. The guidelines of the campaign are deliberately flexible. People can make up their own tally sheets and ways of documenting books read. Generally, though it is our hope that people will have wide access to the enclosed tally sheet. It will make our job a lot easier. Volunteers will meet monthly to tally the results by county. Press releases will go out to local media telling them how your county is doing. Generic ads will be sent to statewide newspapers with a request that they be run on a space available basis through October 14. There will be promotion through the *Rocky Mountain News* and their Newspaper In Education program, as well as other general promotion. There are no rules, and we hope that participants will be creative in urging people to read. The tally forms are ultimately to be returned to the Colorado Center for the Book, 1301 Arapahoe Street, Suite 3, Golden, Co. 80401. If you have questions about Read the Rockies you can direct them to (303) 273-5933 or the e-mail address Snoozzin@aol.com.

Read the Rockies is an outgrowth of the American Association of School Librarians "Count on Reading" campaign. Their challenge is to schools or organizations to test the power of reading initiatives. Anyone who is interested in developing research models to test the power of reading is invited to contact the American Library Association.

As of the press date for the Count on Reading Handbook, the Colorado Center for the Book can be reached by telephone at (303) 839-8320 and by fax at (303) 839-8319.

Read the Rockies, Colorado Style

PROMOTION IDEAS FROM READ THE ROCKIES

The purpose of this section is to give you some ideas of ways you can use the theme to promote reading. Our hope is that you will embrace this campaign as your own and give it your own spin. The most effective way to accomplish that is by tailoring the materials in this packet to whatever works for your organization/business. You may want to put your address and phone number on the tally sheets and bookmarks or create your own. Let people know that this is your event. While ultimately the tally sheets need to be sent to the Colorado Center for the Book, there is no reason that they can't be collected by you first. Create a big "Read the Rockies" thermometer and display it in an appropriate, visible place. Set you own community goal of books read, and color it in as you begin to reach your goal.

- Create a Read the Rockies challenge where you work by creating a giant chart that encourages people to check off the number of books they have read each day/week/month.
- Give out "Read the Rockies" bookmarks at events and urge people to fill them out and send them in.
- Use the theme as an excuse to invite some great Colorado writers, photographers, illustrators to do a reading or autographing. It will provide you with a spring board to get media coverage and to encourage people to keep reading!
- Use any existing promotions you have to encourage your constituents to tally what they are reading. Examples might include a library summer reading program, a bookstore author event, children's performers, book clubs, or any activity where people assemble around something related to books.
- Set up a friendly competition between schools or businesses or radio stations to see who can collect the largest number of tally sheets. Use this to draw attention to your organization's/business's commitment to reading.
- Think of all the ways you can get tally sheets in the hands of the public. Hand them out when people buy something, send them out in mailings, reproduce them for your newsletter, or stuff them in employee paychecks.
- Sponsor a booth or a table at a public event. Hang a sign that says "Read the Rockies." Put the names of all the people whose books are tallied on a giant picture or drawing of Colorado's fourteeners.
- Get film or media students to produce a program for local cable television on "Read the Rockies." Have it translated into different languages and aired on appropriate programming channels.
- Ask your local radio station to produce public service announcements tailored to your community's "Read the Rockies" campaign.
- Have everyone in your business/organization stop what they are doing and read for a period of time one day and tally their time.

Program Materials

PROMOTION IDEAS FROM READ THE ROCKIES (CONTINUED)

- Seek out speaking opportunities at local ethnic business, religious, professional or neighborhood groups, also adult schools, and explain how they can find appropriate books to read and support "Read the Rockies."
- Set up a "Read the Rockies" corner. Create an inviting atmosphere with comfortable chairs and plenty of reading materials including newspapers, magazines, newsletters, books, comic books, etc. Have an attractive sign that explains the simple steps to participate in the promotion. Make sure tally sheets are available.
- Have children contact friends and family to "sign up" to read ten books over a desig- nated period of time. The children can create a record sheet that would have a space for people to initial their commitment to participate. The children can give the participant a tally sheet and promise to return in a designated period of time to collect the sheets.
- Contact a local radio station and arrange for something to be read aloud. All of the people who listen can call in and be counted for the tally.
- Do a "Read the Rockies Marathon" in you business. Line up as many local stars as you can to rotate reading as many books as they can. The "Read the Rockies Marathon" could last for two hours with a goal of reading x number of books. It would encourage people to read short books, articles, etc., to get the count up.
- Challenge another school, business or community to a competition to see who reads the most books for a designated period of time. This could attract great press attention!
- Challenge employees to read their memos and other interoffice communication and get them to tally time spent reading.
- Create stickers that say "I Read the Rockies." Give the stickers to anyone who completes a tally sheet.
- Create a tally sheet that asks people to identify the books they read. Compile the list and offer the media a profile of the most read books in your area/company/organization.
- The sheet of newspaper ads included in this packet are ready to be used for you local newspaper or newsletters.
- Feel free to use the logo and anything else in this packet in any way you choose to adapt it to your promotion.
- **TAKE TEN**! is a promotion we hope everyone will participate in to help us meet this goal. On October 10 at 10 a.m. people everywhere are encouraged to stop what they are doing and read for ten minutes. This is the second year of this promotion. In 1994 Take Ten was observed on Indian reservations, in grocery stores, schools, businesses and just about everywhere people happened to be. There is an extra promotional push for Take Ten so please let us know if you're planning a special observance, so we can help you get press coverage.

21

Read the Rockies, Colorado Style

SAMPLE PRESS RELEASE FROM READ THE ROCKIES

FOR IMMEDIATE RELEASE
COLORADANS "READ THE ROCKIES"

Coloradans will read three million books between now and October 14 if a coalition of reading groups has their way. "Read the Rockies," a campaign launched in April during National Library Week, is designed to keep people of all ages reading.

The campaign encourages everyone from individuals to businesses to get behind the effort. All that's required is that people read anything they want, write down the number of things they've read, and let campaign organizers know. "The impetus for Read the Rockies," said Center for the Book Executive Director Kimberly Taylor, "was a recent study by Stephen Krashen author of *The Power of Reading*. Krashen's premise is that reading is the most powerful tool available for building vocabulary and increasing the ability to read, write, spell, and comprehend. He specifically mentions the value of reading aloud, light reading and nontraditional forms of voluntary reading. Not surprisingly, print-rich environments like the library are crucial for building an audience of readers."

The six-month campaign relies on partnerships with schools, bookstores, restaurants, media, libraries, nursing homes, book clubs, individuals, and businesses to work. The rules are simple. Any reading material can be counted toward the goal. People can read newspapers, brochures, comic books, novels, magazines, annual reports, or anything with printed words. Individual or group tallies can be submitted in any form to the Colorado Center for the Book, 1301 Arapahoe, Suite 3, Golden, Co. 80401. The purpose of this six-month promotion is to build a community of readers by encouraging people at all age levels to read.

Read the Rockies is sponsored by the American Association of School Librarians, Aurora Public Library, Colorado Center for the Book, Colorado Department of Education, Colorado Educational Media Association, Colorado Library Association, Colorado State Library, Denver Public Schools, Libraries Unlimited, *Rocky Mountain News* and the Tattered Cover. Information on National Library Week or how to participate in Read the Rockies is available by calling (303) 273-5933.

###END###

As of the press date for the Count on Reading Handbook, the Colorado Center for the Book can be reached by telephone at (303) 839-8320 and by fax at (303) 839-8319.

Program Materials

Read the Rockies

TIPS FOR DEALING WITH THE MEDIA FROM READ THE ROCKIES

- The best way to meet with success with the media is to call your request in first. They will invite printed information which you can fax or mail. Then, follow up with another phone call. They are very busy and get a lot of requests. Yours will be lost if you simply send a request and wait for a response.

- Make sure you are talking to the person who can help you. If you are asking for news coverage, talk to the editorial side. If your are asking for promotional/advertising space, talk to the advertising side. Give a brief explanation of what you are calling for and ask them to direct you to the appropriate person.

- Newspaper In Education programs are often a good way to get coverage. If your request is related to children, they generally have space they can give you to get the message across.

- Call the advertising people and ask if you can create a space available ad (for newspapers) promoting your project. Your ad will become a filler ad when they have space available that they need to fill. Make sure they give you the dimensions they need.

- Radio stations that do public affairs or news programs are good candidates for Read the Rockies coverage. Often they will say sure and ask you if you are ready right then. Be prepared! You need to suggest the angle to them. The angle is that we are trying to get Coloradans to read three million books, and these are the activities our community has gotten behind to make that happen.

- Don't give up if you are rejected. If you are persistent, eventually the person will tire of turning you down.
- If you can, get to know your targeted media contact personally. Request an information meeting to find out what kind of stories they do, how you can be useful to them, and who the appropriate staff people are for various things.

- Stations/newspapers are inclined to cover activities that their staff is involved in. Make a media person an emcee/judge/personality at your event. It helps!

23

Read the Rockies, Colorado Style

FOR IMMEDIATE RELEASE
Contact: Kimberly Taylor
            (303) 273-5934

COLORADANS READ 3 MILLION BOOKS!

Golden--Colorado residents successfully met a challenge by a coalition of reading groups to read 3 million books in six months. The final tally for the "Read The Rockies" challenge is 3,112,492.

On April 9th a challenge was issued to Coloradans to document their reading and help prove that by October 10th residents could read 3 million books. Tallies came in from every corner of the state. A wide ranging group of people participated including schools, government, businesses, individuals, a correction facility, families and libraries.

"By the end of August, we really thought we had a losing campaign on our hands," said Kimberly Taylor, Director of the Colorado Center for the Book. "We weren't even at one million and we had six weeks to go. They started trickling in in September and by the first two weeks of October, we were inundated with tallies. We heard from individuals and businesses from all corners of the state and most spots in between. People loved it and many of them pleaded with us to repeat it again. We are delighted that the campaign worked and that Coloradans came out in force to demonstrate that we are a state of readers."

--MORE--

As of the press date for the Count on Reading Handbook, the Colorado Center for the Book can be reached by telephone at (303) 839-8320 and by fax at (303) 839-8319.

Program Materials

The anecdotes from the campaign are many. A seventy-six year old couple from Aurora got their tally in just under the wire and it was postmarked Tulsa, Oklahoma. Marjorie Stanley wrote, "Have been traveling and not reading as much-unless road maps count!!" The Stanley's were re' onsible for 63 books between the two of them. The Delta Correctional Facility inmates sent in a tally of 131 books read. Kendallvue Elementary School in Jefferson County sent in a total of 8,005 books read. They got the American Legion involved and really pushed it among their families. Their top family, the Sugar's, read 468 books. Part of the credit for the heavy involvement of the schools goes to the Colorado Department of Education (CDE) where officials not only worked hard to encourage schools to read, but also had their own internal campaign for employees. CDE turned in over 1100 books read.

The impetus for the campaign was a national effort sponsored by the American Association of School Librarians who are in the middle of a "Count on Reading" campaign designed to urge young people to read. Colorado developed a slightly different approach designed to encourage all people to read. Both campaigns cite Stephen Krashen's book *The Power of Reading* as providing compelling evidence that reading is the most powerful tool available for building vocabulary and increasing the ability to read, write, spell, and comprehend. He cites print rich environments like school and public libraries as critical for building an audience of readers.

Read The Rockies is sponsored by the American Association of School Librarians, Aurora Public Library, Colorado Center for the Book, Colorado Department of Education, Colorado Educational Media Association, Colorado Library Association, Colorado State Library, Denver Public Schools, Libraries Unlimited, Rocky Mountain News and the Tattered Cover. The coalition agrees that promotions that stimulate reading are invaluable and plans are underway to launch a similar activity for 1996. People interested in being on the mailing list for these reading initiatives should call (303) 273-5933.

###END###

As of the press date for the Count on Reading Handbook, the Colorado Center for the Book can be reached by telephone at (303) 839-8320 and by fax at (303) 839-8319.

Read the Rockies, Colorado Style

Read the Rockies

A Challenge for All Coloradans to Read Three Million Books by October 10, 1995.

NATIONAL LIBRARY WEEK, 1995

Read the Rockies is an umbrella program that concentrates on developing and keeping the reading habit. It does not replace any reading initiative currently in place — that reading can be counted too. The goal is to build a community of readers in the home, the classroom, the school, the community, and the state.

Who Can Participate?
Everyone — from Babies to Senior Citizens

How?
Read books, magazines, newspapers — or have someone read to you.

Sponsors: Colorado Center for the Book • Colorado State Library and Adult Education Office • Colorado Department of Education • Rocky Mountain News in Education • Tattered Cover • Libraries Unlimited • Colorado Library Association • Colorado Educational Media Association.

Find out more about Read the Rockies!
• •

Please send the Read the Rockies kit to:

Name_____
Agency _____
Address _____
City, Zip _____

Return this form to the Libraries Unlimited Booth and your kit will be mailed to you in mid-February. Or Mail to: Read the Rockies • Colorado Center for the Book • 1301 Arapahoe Street, Suite 3 • Golden, CO 80401. For more information call: (303) 273-5933 or Fax (303) 273-5935

As of the press date for the Count on Reading Handbook, the Colorado Center for the Book can be reached by telephone at (303) 839-8320 and by fax at (303) 839-8319.

Program Materials

Won't You Join Us?
Read! Read! Read!

We want to prove that Colorado is a community of readers. Our goal? Three million books read between now and October 10th.

To make your reading count, visit your local library for information on how you can participate.

Sponsors: Colorado Center for the Book, Colorado State Library and Adult Education Office, Libraries Unlimited, Tattered Cover, Rocky Mountain News in Education, Denver Public Schools, Aurora Public Library, Colorado Library Association, Colorado Educational Media Association and your local library.

Won't You Join Us?
Read! Read! Read!

We want to prove that Colorado is a community of readers. Our goal? Three million books read between now and October 10th.

To make your reading count, visit your local library for information on how you can participate.

Sponsors: Colorado Center for the Book, Colorado State Library and Adult Education Office, Libraries Unlimited, Tattered Cover, Rocky Mountain News in Education, Denver Public Schools, Aurora Public Library, Colorado Library Association, Colorado Educational Media Association and your local library.

27

Won't You Join Us?
Read! Read! Read!

We want to prove that Colorado is a community of readers. Our goal? Three million books read between now and October 10th.

To make your reading count, visit your local library for information on how you can participate.

Sponsors: Colorado Center for the Book, Colorado State Library and Adult Education Office, Libraries Unlimited, Tattered Cover, Rocky Mountain News In Education, Denver Public Schools, Aurora Public Library, Colorado Library Association, Colorado Educational Media Association and your local library.

Read the Rockies, Colorado Style - Program Materials

Your Reading Counts!

Help us count what you've read.
Fill out the back and send it in.

Colorado
Read the Rockies

List the books you have read, then send to:

Read the Rockies
Colorado Center for the Book
1301 Arapahoe, Suite 3
Golden, CO 80401
(Please send in by October 10, 1995.)

Building Reading Roads to the Information Highway

First in the Nation!

Even before the National

Count on Reading Initiative

was underway, two New

Susan C. Snider

COUNT ON READING
Building Reading Roads To The Information Highway

Hampshire librarians, Susan Ballard, director of library, media and technology services for the

Londonderry School District, and Betty O'Donnell, adult services librarian for Manchester City

Library, established a steering committee consisting of a diverse group of librarians and other educa-

tors to explore ways for New Hampshire to develop and implement a state reading initiative and

provide leadership to the rest of the country. Included in the group were an elementary school princi-

pal, and librarians representing schools and public libraries, the state library, and the department of

education. Both Susan, then a member of the AASL Board of Directors, and Betty, then President

of the Young Adult Library Services Association (YALSA), a division of the American Library

Association, were well informed about the dream that AASL Past Presidents Blanche Woolls and

David Loertscher shared in developing a national reading initiative, and they successfully ignited the

group with their enthusiasm.

Steering Committee Organization and Activities

Even though New Hampshire understood the concepts of AASL's Count on Reading effort, the group decided to create a sense of ownership for a state initiative. They developed the following mission statement:

"The mission of Count on Reading is to promote the intrinsic value of reading."

Developing such a short statement took much longer than one might imagine! The group was familiar with the research of Stephen Krashen and used his book, *The Power of Reading*, as a guide. Recognizing that the more kids read

voluntarily, the more they just plain read, it was realized that New Hampshire needed to focus on promoting the idea of reading for reading's sake, not for an extrinsic incentive as many other programs do.

Once the mission and goals were established, the group began to work on details and to define some specifics regarding the "who's" and "how's." Flyers and brochures were developed to help promote and explain the initiative and to provide suggestions for local activities. Forms for collecting the school data and for collecting state data to send to the national initiative were designed, and a rule of thumb to help teachers and librarians decide what counted as "a book" was developed. A graphic artist was hired to design a logo that contained all of the required elements: a local identity, reading, and the information age theme.

The group debated and debated about the challenge it would present to New Hampshire readers. The state goal would be based on how many books it would take to reach the northern most corner of New Hampshire from the Massachusetts border. It was more difficult to decide whether to determine the number by counting the books as though they were standing up as if on a shelf, or, as if they were lying down, end to end. While David Loertscher suggested that using 23 million books as a goal (books standing up) it was decided to begin with a smaller goal of 1,140,480 books (lying down, end to end).

Hoping for this project to generate as much participation as possible, the committee encouraged any school, public library, organization or community group to become involved. Local activities were encouraged. They included:

- Developing local goals such as reading across the classroom, down the hall, out the door, down the block and on to a wider community goal;

- Challenging other classrooms, schools, and communities;

- Developing school and public library partnerships, public school and daycare and nursery school partnerships, or any kind of community partnership;

- Developing a Count on Reading column or providing a press release for coverage in the local and school newspapers.

The Five:One Ratio Rule

Reading for the intrinsic value of reading means reading anything in any format. Anticipating questions about how much certain formats should count, the group developed the Five:One Ratio Rule which establishes the following guideline:

- five magazines = one book

- five articles = one magazine

- five newspapers = one book

- five sections = one newspaper

- five comic books = one book

Local communities determined if a book the length of *Moby Dick* was to count the same as a book the length of the *Red Pony*.

Recruiting Project Partners

Recognizing the need to reach the broader education community, the presidents of numerous educational and community organizations were invited to attend a tea where the initiative would be explained and promoted. Approximately forty people attended the event, including a legislator and representatives from the statewide school volunteers association, Granite State Reading Council, New Hampshire Principals Association, Retired Teachers Association, American Association of Retired Persons, the Business and Professional Women's Association, New Hampshire Educational Media Association, New Hampshire Library Association, School Board Association, and School Administrator's Association. Each attendee received a packet of materials that explained New Hampshire Count on Reading and included an article for their organizations' newsletter. Entertainment was provided by a team of two of the steering committee members who did a choral reading of a story they developed to explain the initiative. The gathering was a great success and ended with all present signing on as partners.

31

Continued on next page

Building Reading Roads to the Information Highway

Launching the Project

New Hampshire Count on Reading was officially launched in April 1994 by David Loertscher at the New Hampshire Educational Media Association annual conference. In June, a mailing that included a registration form and start-up materials was sent to all school and public libraries. Public libraries began "the count," during that summer. In the fall, school librarians throughout the state launched initiatives. New Hampshire began to tally numbers to contribute to the national count.

Procedures for "the count" were developed to make it as easy as possible for teachers and librarians at the local level.

Each month teachers sent their monthly book counts to the school librarian, who combined them and sent them on to the member of the state steering committee, who combined the school and public library report and sent them on to AASL. Including a space for sharing information on the monthly reporting form was a quick and easy way for busy librarians to communicate what was happening at the local sites. A follow-up call provided more details when necessary. This news and information was shared with the rest of the state through the Count on Reading Newsletter that was distributed with the state organization's newsletter. It was

exciting to hear what others were doing and to have been able to share that information. One elementary school librarian launched Count on Reading in her school in a school-wide assembly where fourth graders presented a skit called the *Reading Rap*. It was such a success that they traveled to other schools to perform.

In April 1995, the reading goal for the state was met. This happened before the committee could, as planned, erect a large plywood map of the state on the State Library lawn, that showed how New Hampshire's youth were reading their way up the "Information Highway" represented by Interstate 93.

Conclusions and a Recommendations Checklist

■ **Adopt or adapt good ideas** — When you are ready to take on a long-term reading incentive project, use the ideas that New Hampshire and other states have used to develop your own initiative. While it is extremely important to develop ownership for your own project, you don't have to start from scratch. Strongest recommendations include:

– Have a broad base of representation on the steering committee.

– Be sure to include at least one administrator. The principal on the New Hampshire committee was very important in providing a fresh perspective and in making connections that might not have been made without her.

■ **Market the program to *all* educational groups.** Involve them in as many ways as possible. New Hampshire did not seek financial support from its partners. They were good-will partners who helped spread the word to their members.

■ **Maintain as much local control as possible.** Provide guidelines and suggestions, but remain flexible.

■ **Develop simple procedures for reporting.** This is crucial.

■ **Develop visible ways to keep the public informed.** A logo used on all press releases and documentation is essential…and feel free to use the New Hampshire state map idea to show your progress!

■ **Bring new members on board to carry the initiative forward after it has been launched.** It is easy to run out of steam when so much energy is expended at the outset. Initial excitement needs to be revived with the addition of new people as the initiative evolves. Fresh energy is revitalizing.

■ **Find a vehicle for sharing information and for bringing new groups into the project.** New Hampshire used a newsletter. Others may choose a Web site.

■ **Finally, learn from our mistake and set your reading goal high.** Although the original state goal was met earlier than anticipated, "New Hampshire Count on Reading" continues. Youth are now challenged to reach the goal of 23 million books that David Loertscher so wisely suggested in the beginning!

33

Susan C. Snider is an education consultant for the Office of Research and Development for the New Hampshire State Department of Education in Concord, New Hampshire. She is a member of the New Hampshire Count on Reading State Steering Committee.

COUNT ON READING
Building Reading Roads To
The Information Highway

MISSION

The mission of Count on Reading is to promote the intrinsic value of reading.

GOALS AND OBJECTIVES

To increase the impact of modeling in the reading process. (model)

- the community will participate in school and library settings

- families will read together

- adults will demonstrate the value of reading

To increase the amount of free voluntary reading (FVR) by students. (quantity)

- educators and librarians will make students aware of the volume of FVR

- adults will encourage participation in reading activities

- activities and incentives will be provided to promote FVR

To add a local component to the existing body of research evidence which documents the impact of FVR (research)

- a research project will be designed and conducted

- data will be gathered and evaluated

- results will be disseminated

To create attitudes which sustain reading as a lifelong activity. (attitude)

- students will attain success through reading

- students will read for the love of it!

Program Materials

COUNT ON READING
Building Reading Roads To
The Information Highway

A Challenge to the Youth of New Hampshire
To Read at least 1,140,480 Books

Major Activities:

Establish reading initiative/build on existing ones to achieve the state
reading goal (enough books laid end to end to stretch the length of the state)

Promote school and public library cooperative efforts

Tally the number of books read by the youth of New Hampshire

Celebrate goal achievement – more reading, better writing, higher achievement

Proposed State Committee Activities:

Regular press releases

Arrange for "Celebrity Visits

Provide Basic Information/Reporting Forms

Develop Suggested Support Strategies

Identify/Recognize Successful Efforts

Collect/Analyze/Disseminate Statistics

35

Building Reading Roads to the Information Highway

COUNT ON READING
Building Reading Roads To
The Information Highway

PRESENTATION DIALOG

We've all heard the talk about it -- the information highway, the NII the National Information Infrastructure. But what is it and what does it have to do with reading and books?

The hype is that the information highway will "enable the widespread use of a remarkable set of telecommunications, computing and interactive applications that will change business, entertainment, and personal life worldwide.[1]

The actual information highway is described in a 1993 Business Week article as "broadband networks -- high speed, high-performance supercomputers with an array of wireless links, satellite relays and fiber optic cables to feed data, voice, and video images into the same coaxial cables and copper wires that constitute most of today's home and office communication infrastructure."[2] (A real mouthful!)

Sounds pretty exciting, right? Sounds pretty complicated too. Maybe even a little intimidating. And how do we gain access to the information highway? What constitutes a driver's license?

It's not jus the right technology and access codes. It's the ability to read, to compute, to comprehend and think critically, to spell and use grammar correctly. Many of New Hampshire's children are in danger of failing this important driver's test -- without a little help from the rest of us.

When navigating the information highway, a student's success rides on his or her ability to access, analyze and read data. "Read" is the key word. Computers and databases produce information in full-text print. you have to read it to understand it. "In short, if you can't read well and apply what you read, then no computer that's going to be available in our lifetime will help you much."[3]

But information isn't a new idea -- what is **new** is a labyrinthian network of data many of us may have trouble untangling. Improved access to this data is brought about through technology. And with new technology often comes upheaval and stress.

Everyone can recall their first encounter with a computer, whether it was a video game call Pong, learning how to do an ERIC search or trying to plug in the new computer you just purchased for a family Christmas present. There are feelings of confusion, ineptitude, sometimes panic, and ultimately (we hope) excitement and growing confidence.

The Count on Reading Program will help steer children in the right direction, instilling confidence by improving literacy skills and exciting them about reading. Improved literacy skills will help alleviate some of the stress associated with new technologies.

While in some communities children are bottle-fed on new technology and become more computer-literate than many of us, a lot of families and communities are still playing catch up.

For instance, did you know that there are more than 75,000 adults in New Hampshire who lack the basic reading and math skills to accomplish everyday tasks -- like filling out a job application, reading a recipe or counting their change at the supermarket? Many adults can't understand the simple computerized instructions at a bank cash machine. These adults will fail the information highway driver's text and so will their children, if we don't help.

Program Materials

How can we help? Well, ask yourself how many books have you read recently? How much time do you spend reading newspapers, book, magazines? The average adult American reads just <u>24 minutes</u> a day.[4] It's easier to switch on a TV to watch Beavis and Butthead or play Mortal Kombat than it is to pick up a book.

More than 2/3 of households with school-age children have two parents working outside the home. After working a full day, getting a meal on the table, helping children with homework, and zoning out in front of the TV for an hour or two, the typical American parent ends up devoting less than 1 1/2 hours a day to child care, according to a study done by the University of Maryland.[5] A harried parent doesn't have much time to read, not for themselves, not to their children.

"Should anyone care if our nation isn't reading? After all -- people get information from television, radio, video cassettes, and audio tapes. Workers can learn their jobs by attending a class or putting a tape in the VCR. Computer databases give you more facts than you'll ever need and CNN tells you what's happening in the world. Who needs to read?

The answer is anyone who hopes to be productive and successful. Reading is linked to many of the important skills needed to succeed in today's world -- among them speech and writing."[6]

Educators agree that the greatest predictor of scholastic achievement is the time parents spend reading to their children. Children who are read to become readers. It is as simple as that.

Parents and teachers reading aloud to children --valuing recreational reading as well as homework and sports -- these are the efforts that are going to help bring New Hampshire's children to the skill level they need to pass that driver's test and become active, successful users of the technology of today and the future.

Count on Reading will build the access roads for New Hampshire's children by promoting the intrinsic value of reading to children, to their parents, to teachers and to librarians. We will encourage adults to make reading an everyday habit in the homes and in the schools. We will increase time spent reading by initiating reading challenges -- to children, schools and communities.

What will the results of the Count on Reading initiative be? Our children will become better readers and their vocabularies will improve. They will think more critically and write more clearly. Their future travels on the information highway will be successful and productive. All this will come true if we can excite children about reading.

But if we as a nation increasingly disregard the printed word (24 minutes a day, that's kind of pitiful), if we devalue reading by not making it an important part of our own households, the effects could be chilling. "In a world filled with TV screens, movies and music, our children are already losing the interest and ability to read.'"[7]

Unless we start reading more, our children may some day lose their ability to discern worlds different from the ones already created for them on the computer screen. The philosopher Ludwig Wittgenstein said, the limits of our language are the limits of our world. Count on reading to take you to other worlds. Count on us to get you started.

Sources Cited

1. "Information Highways 1993: The Computerization of Business and Society." **Business Week** (Nov. 29, 1993): 95.

2. "Information Highways 1993: The Computerization of Business and Society." **Business Week** (Nov. 29, 1993): 95–96.

3. "It's Reading, Stupid!" **Scholastic Library Media Activities Monthly**, (Nov. 1993): 4.

4. "America Won't Win Till It Reads More" **Fortune**, (Nov. 18, 1991): 201.

5. "America Won't Win Till It Reads More" **Fortune**, (Nov. 18, 1991): 204.

6. "America Won't Win Till It Reads More" **Fortune**, (Nov. 18, 1991): 202.

7. "When We Get the Libraries We Want, Will We Want the Libraries We Get?" **Wilson Library Bulletin**, (June 1991): 31.

37

COUNT ON READING
Building Reading Roads To
The Information Highway

Count on Reading
Registration Form

Yes, we would like to be a member of the **Count on Reading** Initiative.

Contact Person: _____

Title: _____

School/Library: _____

Address: _____

_____

Telephone: _____

Return this form to:

Heidi Webster, Count on Reading
Indian River School
RR 1 Box 169
Canaan, NH 03741

New Hampshire Count on Reading is a state project supporting the national
Count on Reading initiative, a project of the American Association of School
Librarians, a division of the American Library Association.

Program Materials

COUNT ON READING
Building Reading Roads To
The Information Highway

Count on Reading
Monthly Report

Contact Person: _____

School/Library: _____

This report is for the month of _____, 199____

_____ # of participants

_____ # of books (or book equivalents) read

> Guidelines: "The Five = One Rule"
> 5 magazines = 1 book   5 articles = 1 magazine
> 5 newspapers = 1 book   5 sections = 1 newspaper
> 5 comic books = 1 book

Comments/successes, news for the state committee:

MAIL TO:

Heidi Webster, Count on Reading
Indian River School
RR 1 Box 169
Canaan, NH 03741

39

Building Reading Roads to the Information Highway

Kay Klein, Library Media Specialist at Peter Woodbury and Memorial School in Bedford, introduced students to the Count on Reading program at an assembly program using the READING RAP...We've received permission to reprint it here and Kay invites you to adapt the activity for your own situations.

DIG THIS!

THE READING RAP

We're here today with something to say
We want you to read books every day.

We'll build a road clear 'cross the state
So let's get started and we won't be late.

Construction Man is here right now
To get you started and to show you how.

Hey, "C" Man, come right on through
Tell us all what we need to do.

READ, READ. HELP CARRY THE LOAD.
READ, READ. WE'LL BUILD THE READING ROAD.

Wait, Mr. C., don't get uptight.
We don't think that you've got it all right.

We don't want a road goin' on the floor.
We don't want a road out the door.

Our kind of road goes in your head.
You do it every night before you go to bed.

Well, Mr. C., you've got your two-by-four.
Just sit right down and we'll show you more.

READ, READ. HELP CARRY THE LOAD.
READ, READ. WE'LL BUILD THE READING ROAD.

"To" means someone else reads to you -
Mom, Dad, Sister - even brother will do.

"By" is when you read all by yourself.
Just pick up any book you find on your shelf.

"For" means that you read for each other.
Read for your Aunt, your Dad or your Mother.

Fill up the form and bring it back to school.
You may win a prize and that'd be cool!

READ, READ. HELP CARRY THE LOAD.
READ, READ. WE'LL BUILD THE READING ROAD.

40

Program Materials

COUNT ON READING
Building Reading Roads To The Information Highway

NEWS/UPDATES -MAY/JUNE 1995

1,222,334 BOOKS READ AND COUNTING!!

It may come as a surprise to some, but not to those who know how much NH kids loves to read, that we have surpassed our original goal of reading 1,140,480 books. We did it a relatively short period of time and we did it without all the numbers in that we know are out there!! So let's keep reading NH!! And let's resolve to do a better job of checking in with our results. At one point we had considered reading twenty three million books and if we all report faithfully, we can reach that number in no time. In turn, the Count on Reading Committee will try and do a better job of staying in touch with you!

New Hampshire has bragging rights when it comes to the national count as well!! As of now, we account for 45% of the books reported!! In our state, **Bedford** wins the "Town that Can't Stop Reading" Award. In a mirror fashion, Bedford accounts for 45% of the NH count! Congratulations to the **Bedford Public Library, the Peter Woodbury School, Memorial School and McKelvie Middle School** You are our Reading Heroes and a model of the cooperative spirit that exists between libraries!!

Bedford is by no means alone when it comes to reporting good news. We have exciting developments throughout the state and hope all of participants can take a page from the books of several other successful programs. Here's just a sampling of what is happening in other communities: Students at the **Maple Avenue Elementary School in Goffstown** are building a "Yellow Brick reading Road" They add a brick for every 100 books read and they may give Bedford a run for the money! **North Londonderry School** is racing down Mammoth Road and chart their progress with some funky cars which move a measured amount on a representative bulletin board. Several schools in Nashua, including the **Main Dunstable Elementary and Charlotte Avenue** are reporting great success with their programs.. Charlotte

Avenue, was formally adopted by the local Saturn Corporation and students are reading their way to the store! People from Saturn, have visited the school to read aloud to classes and help with the cause! Meanwhile students at the **Indian River Middle School in Canaan** are reading their way up Cardigan Mountain! Progress is reported monthly in a library display and at last report, they were more than halfway to their goal! And at the **Hollis Brookline Junior High School**, students count their SSR (sustained, silent reading time) toward their contribution to the state goal. **Concord Schools** have a great idea and are sending representative "feet" for each book read to be displayed at the Concord Public Library!! In **Merrimack**, the kids are counting on their school library media specialists who come up with imaginative, seasonal bulletin board to reflect the numbers of books read. We'd love to report more good news so keep us informed of your successes.

Count on Reading Committee
Susan Ballard, Londonderry School District (Co-Chair)
Betty O'Donnell, , Manchester City Library (Co-Chair)

Becky Albert, NH Council on Literacy, NH State Library
Jean Grout, NHLA (YA's), Exeter Public Library
Connie Ross, GSRC/IRA, South Londonderry School
Becky Shultz, NHLA/CHILIS, Bates Library, Hopkinton
Susan C. Snider, NH State Department of Education
Heidi Webster, NHeima, Indian River School, Canaan
Kendall F. Wiggin, State Librarian

Registration/Reporting/Information

send registration and reports to Heidi Webster, Indian River Middle School , RR 1, Box 169 Canaan, NH 03741

for a registration/information package contact Sue Ballard,Londonderry School District, 268 Mammoth Road, Londonderry, NH 03053
(603) 432-6920/sballard@a1.reg.seresc.k12.nh.us

41

Connecticut Kids Count on Reading

Shelly Senator

Connecticut Kids Count on Reading
And Connecticut Counts on Kids

Connecticut Kids Count on Reading had its first organizational meeting in January 1995. The steering committee represented groups in Connecticut concerned with children, reading and literacy, libraries and education. The committee was composed of representatives of the Connecticut Library Association, the Connecticut Council of Teachers of English, the Connecticut Reading Association, the Connecticut State Department of Education, the Connecticut State Library, and the Connecticut Educational Media Association, which is an AASL affiliate.

First Things First

Our first task was to write a mission statement and goals:

Mission

To challenge the young people of Connecticut to discover the pleasure and value of reading.

Goals and Objectives

To foster lifelong reading habits (attitude)

- by demonstrating the importance of reading to living and working in our society
- by providing students with successful and enjoyable reading experiences

To increase the reading of all Connecticut youth (quantity)

- through encouraging regular, sustained, silent reading at school and daily home reading
- through encouraging participation in reading activities and to provide suggested activities

- through promoting greater access to books and other reading material for all students
- through the sharing of activities that promote reading

To provide models of the value and enjoyment of reading (model)

- by inviting the community to participate in school and library settings
- by challenging families to read together
- by encouraging adults to demonstrate and share the value of reading in their own lives

To invite action research by interested groups or individuals (research)

Developing Materials

The committee developed its own state name and logo. The name chosen was Connecticut Kids Count on Reading and Connecticut Counts on Kids. Our state logo was the national Count on Reading logo with the outline of Connecticut added.

The steering committee decided that Connecticut should have a state-wide program that included direct reporting of the count by the participants to the state organization. This would allow monitoring of whether or not the state was reaching every town in the state and to keep a Connecticut count of the books read. There are 169 towns in Connecticut, and one of the objectives was to have the participation of each town in the state. To provide an incentive, a 4' x 8' signboard map of Connecticut that showed each town outlined on the map was designed. In the registration materials, it was promised to affix a red star to the map that designated participation by a town. Participants were told that the map would be prominently displayed in the state library in Hartford, the state capitol.

Alongside the map would be an up-to-date listing of each individual (school, library) site within that town so that all participants would be known. This was a very effective way of signing-on participants. Classroom teachers and library media specialists have written us saying that they will bring their students to the capitol in order to see their town's star proudly displayed on the map.

Setting a Reading Goal and Getting the Project Started

As part of our contribution to the national goal of a billion books, a state-wide long-term goal of 2,471,070 books to be read was set. The goal was to read around the perimeter of the state of Connecticut (ten inch books laid end-to-end). A flyer that encouraged participation and registration was designed, written, and distributed state-wide to the members of various organizations.

Plans called for the state program to begin as soon as possible. The idea was to capitalize on the children's summer reading programs that are conducted by the public libraries throughout the state. School library media centers were encouraged to sign up by the beginning of the upcoming school year in order to increase or expand reading incentive programs. Committee meetings had begun in January, and the first mailing of publicity and registration materials was in April. The official kick-off event was held the following November.

A Big Send-Up

The AASL state affiliate, the Connecticut Educational Media Association (CEMA), had its state conference in November, and the committee decided to launch its initiative at this conference. A brochure was designed, a list of professional organizations that might be aligned within a reading initiative was constructed, and invitations to a two-hour informational gala were sent to all organizations. Scheduling this event just before the preconference for CEMA would allow the inclusion of many of the library media specialists and other teachers who attended. The speakers at this "kick off" session were inspirational and informative; AASL Past President David Loertscher was among them. He spoke to the audience about the importance of free voluntary reading in the lives of children.

As promised in the original mailing, the self-standing, four-by-eight-foot map of Connecticut, complete with outlines of the towns and a legend indicating which were "participating towns" was on display. Each town was represented by a two-inch red vinyl star with the town's name clearly printed on it. Alongside

Continued on next page

43

Connecticut Kids Count on Reading

this map was a list of all the participating schools, libraries, and individuals within each town. This certainly proved to be an incentive to promote registration. In order to publicize Connecticut Kids Count on Reading, a table that had registration packets and other materials was set up. The map was on display there, too. The governor's recent proclamation on Count on Reading was distributed to all registrants, as well. During the conference, Margaret Queenan, a steering committee member and then president of Connecticut Council of Teachers of English, conducted a workshop, the theme of which was, "How to Conduct Action Research." One of our stated goals is to invite action research, and Dr. Queenan's workshop fulfilled a need for those practitioners who were interested in learning about this.

Staying Connected through Communications

At the conference, the first newsletter was distributed to the membership and all registered participants. In the newsletter was a graph indicating progress towards the goal, information about the national initiative (end date, national count), information about sponsors, and several success stories from around the state. Examples from elementary and secondary school libraries, as well as public libraries, were included. The newsletter was an important piece of the Connecticut state initiative. Responses from the newsletter included letters, newspaper articles, count sheets with numerous notes and comments. One came from a child who was filling out his own count sheet. He had taken a count sheet from his local public library and initialed a box each time he finished a number of magazines, newspapers or books. He had written on the top of the completed sheet, "It took a while, but I did it!"

The newsletter was an important part of the Connecticut program because it allowed communication with our members, to tell them about what is happening in other towns, and to share ideas among participants. The most frequent request received was for ideas to encourage and increase the reading done by their children.

The newsletter was just one of the items that the committee hoped to supply to participants. A state poster and bookmarks were planned. Because this required funds, solicitation letters were sent to prominent Connecticut corporations, asking for donations to pay for these items. At this writing, four businesses are underwriting the poster, bookmarks, and newsletters. One of them, BIC Corporation has even given over 2,000 pens with the logo on them for participants.

The committee asked one of Connecticut's famous children's authors, Steven Kellogg, to design a bookmark for children who are part of Connecticut Kids Count on Reading. He created a beautiful bookmark, complete with many of his characters (including Pinkerton, the mischievous dog) that was sent to our members. One of the librarians in the state has designed the state poster.

Challenges and How to Meet Them

A reading initiative such as this faces two big challenges. One relates to Count on Reading; the other is a matter of convincing professionals that free voluntary reading makes a difference. The challenge for Count on Reading is to get the word out to those who are not registered. In order to do this, messages have been posted on Internet listservs, LM_NET and KIDLIT_L, articles have been written and reminders have been sent that appear in all the various newsletters that steering committee members represent. (There is an extra benefit of having steering members from both school and public libraries, from English and reading teachers groups, and from the state library and department of education; each group has its own constituency.) Registration materials, state map, and past newsletters were distributed at each state organization meeting throughout the year. Press releases have been sent to radio stations and committee members appeared on the local cable channel in a discussion of Count on Reading.

Promoting Free Voluntary Reading

Promoting free voluntary reading is a more difficult task. The steering committee has a collection of books, articles, and anecdotes related to the importance of encouraging kids to read by giving them the time, space, and material to read. Some of these were included in each of the newsletters. Presenters also talked about the importance of free voluntary reading and mentioned Stephen Krashen's research during staff development activities with other job-alike members. One of the most promising activities was a literacy promotion in conjunction with a country music radio station that is transmitted throughout the state. Country 92.5 was interested in promoting reading. The committee sent them some background material, including Krashen's research, and names of places to visit where they could see the impact of library programs that promoted and supported free voluntary reading. The radio station representatives visited a public library, an elementary school library, and a high school library media center on a once a week basis. They talked to the children involved, worked with them, read to them, discussed books with them. After each visit, they talked about the experience on the radio for the next few days. The committee arranged for them to meet and talk with practitioners, people who were well able to articulate the effectiveness of why and how they do what they do. This was an excellent way of educating the public about the importance of reading and the importance of books and libraries in their lives. Country 92.5 also encouraged parents to sign their children on to long-term reading by joining Connecticut Kids Count on Reading. One of the committee members, Betty Goyette from the state department of education, has written an eight-page booklet about how to encourage reading preschoolers, middle-grade children and teenagers. This booklet will be available to parents who request it. It will also be distributed through the public library and to any school that requests it.

45

Connecticut Kids Count on Reading

Looking Ahead

The committee continues to look to its mission statement and goals to set the course for Connecticut Kids Count on Reading. The steering committee hopes to bring all of the organizations together either to bring Stephen Krashen to the state for a combined conference to discuss the implications of his research findings or to arrange for a teleconference. The committee cheers on the participants in whatever way it can. When an opportunity presents itself, reading or Connecticut Kids Count on Reading is promoted. Above all, Connecticut wants everyone to keep on reading!

Shelly Senator is an educational consultant and author of Collaborations for Literacy: Creating an Integrated Language Arts Program for Middle School (*Greenwood, 1995*). *She is the state coordinator of Connecticut Kids Count on Reading, the Connecticut initiative, representing the Connecticut Educational Media Association. Senator is a member of the National Count on Reading Task Force and editor of the* Count on Reading Update.

Program Materials

76

Connecticut Kids Count on Reading

And Connecticut Counts on Kids

Reading Activities to Encourage Reading

- Challenge another class, grade level, school, or town to a reading contest.
- Read from one classroom or school or library to another (For each book read, count 10" or the length of a
- book.)
- Create a paper link for each book read. Stretch the connected links between classrooms, schools, or libraries.
- Ask the principal to set the challenge and promise to do something special if students reach the goal.
- Create a cheering squad to cheer the readers.
- Drop everything and read (D.E.A.R) whenever a pre-established signal is given.
- Read aloud to a class.
- Replace Power Rangers with power readers.
- Ask physical education teacher to promote the slogan: "Exercise your body; exercise your brain."
- Establish reading buddies among classmates, older schoolmates, and family members.
- Read the distance to the public library, another town, or a special site.
- Read the length of a road and rename the road "Reading Road."
- Link your library/school reading program to Summer Reading Program, School Library Media Month, Night of a Thousand Stars, Nutmeg Book Award, National Library Week.
- Publicize on Open School Night, in monthly reports to the newspaper, and in PTA/Library newsletters.
- Involve the entire district/town in Sustained Silent Reading (SSR).
- "Read around the school/library." Affix a label to the wall for every book read.
- Organize "Read-in's" And "Read-to's" (school, community, parents, homebound).
- Read a book with a partner and respond together.
- Have young people create ways to intrigue younger and older people to read.
- Share/borrow books.
- Take a field trip to the bookroom or library to select "the" book.
- Organize book talks (by students, teachers, librarians, principals, parents, community members!
- Encourage the school and local community to donate favorite books to a student, classroom, or school.
- Invite guests to read to a class (parents, grandparents, school secretary, custodians, superintendent, principal.)
- Bring older and younger students together to read books to each other. Give bookmarks to students autographed by the reader.
- Turn off the TV and read instead.
- Organize a brown bag lunch in the library. Read to students as they eat.
- Provide a supply of magazines for the school cafeteria so students can read as they eat.
- Invite contributions of books on CD Rom so students can read at the computer screen.
- Encourage reluctant readers to read magazine and newspaper articles at the computer screen.
- Create a Reader's Workshop where students read books of their choice in class and write responses which are read and answered by the teacher and other students. Read Nancie Atwell's *In the Middle* for ideas.
- Start a R.E.A.D. club (Reading for Enjoyment and Discussion). Interested students read and recommend books to the student body. They conduct booktalks, interview other students and teachers about reading habits (Linda Walker in *The Book Report*, January/February 1992).
- Start a million page project. The entire school or library population reads until they have reached the goal of 1.000.000 pages read. They then celebrate. (Mary Weil, West School, New Canaan, CT.)

Send us your ideas. We will share them with others!

Connecticut Kids Count on Reading

C o n n e c t i c u t   K i d s
C o u n t   o n   R e a d i n g

And Connecticut Counts on Kids

Please join Connecticut Kids Count on Reading!

Please join us in a statewide Connecticut Kids Count on Reading challenge to Connecticut's young people to read around the perimeter of the state (2,471,070 books) as part of a national Count on Reading goal to read a billion books. We want to help our young people develop a lifetime reading habit, become avid readers, and earn their driver's license for the information superhighway. By linking reading initiatives throughout the state and nation, Count on Reading will have a long-term impact on the reading habits of Connecticut's children.

What is our mission?
  *To challenge the young people of Connecticut to discover the pleasure and value of reading.
What are our goals?
  *To foster lifelong reading habits
  *To increase the reading of all Connecticut youth
  *To show the value of reading
  *To invite action research by those interested

Why should you participate?
  Helping to create a love of reading is the greatest gift you can give to children. Avid reading provides the best chance to succeed in the information society.
Who can participate?
  Any school, public library, organization, or community group can participate. Connecticut Kids Count on Reading will succeed in communities where a number of groups band together to create a long-term reading challenge.
How can you encourage reading?
  Continue the reading initiatives you have already started (DEAR, SSR, summer reading programs, Battle of the Books, National Family Reading Week, read aloud, share a book, create a project.) Read across the room, down the hall, to the public library, and around the perimeter of Connecticut.
How do you get started?
  For every book your children read have them initial a box on the Connecticut Kids Count on Reading Book Count Chart and send the completed chart to Connecticut Kids Count on Reading, 25 Elmwood Ave., Trumbull, CT 06611. If you have statistics from reading initiatives within the last two school years, send them as well. We will use the numbers to help us attract attention to reading in the state and nationwide. For every town that joins us, we will paint a star on the Connecticut State map at the State Library in Hartford.

Program Materials

Connecticut Kids
Count on Reading

And Connecticut Counts on Kids

Connecticut Kids Count on Reading Registration Form

Yes, I would like to be a member of the Connecticut Kids Count on Reading Initiative.

Name:
Organization/School/Library:
Address:

City, State Zip:
Telephone:

_____Please send me ideas to encourage Connecticut children to read.
_____Please send me information on ways to turn my reading motivation program into an action research project.

Return form to Connecticut Kids Count on Reading, 25 Elmwood Ave., Trumbull, CT. 06611.

(Send your filled-in Book Count Charts or number of books read to the above address also.)

Connecticut Kids Count on Reading Initiative Steering Committee:

Susan Cormier, Connecticut State Library 1-800-427-2313
Jan Day, Connecticut Library Association 389-3433
Betty Goyette, State Department of Education 566-6660
Margaret Queenan, Ct. Council of Teachers of English 977-4739
Cynthia Seastrong, Ct. Reading Association 576-7553
Shelly Senator, State Coordinator, Ct. Eductional Media Association 847-2310

Oklahoma's Project Unique: I'd Sooner Read!

Anne Masters

*T*he Oklahoma Count on Reading Task Force held its first meeting in June 1995. Invited to participate were representatives of schools, public libraries, literacy programs, and organizations that support reading and literacy efforts. Members of the Oklahoma Task Force represent the Oklahoma Library for the Blind, the Oklahoma Reading Association, the office of the Governor, the Oklahoma Association of School Library Media Specialists, representatives of public libraries and public schools, the state Literacy Office, the Oklahoma Department of Libraries, Oklahoma's public television station, the Oklahoma Library Association, the Oklahoma State Department of Education, and the Daily Oklahoman. Other members are Kim Doner, award winning children's book illustrator, and Molly Levite Griffis, local author and publisher.

Organizational Efforts

As planning continued, we recruited organizations to sponsor and endorse the project. Sponsoring organizations are the Oklahoma Association of School Library Media Specialists, the Oklahoma Congress of Parents and Teachers, the Oklahoma Department of Libraries, the Oklahoma Literacy Council, and the Oklahoma State Department of Education. Sponsoring organizations have contributed financial support to the project. Endorsing organizations are the Oklahoma Association of Elementary School Principals,

Oklahoma Association of School Administrators, Oklahoma Association of Secondary School Principals, Oklahoma Council for Social Studies, Oklahoma Library Association, the Oklahoma Reading Association, and the University of Oklahoma School of Library and Information Studies.

Initially there was a great deal of discussion about the purpose of the project and concern about duplication of effort. In August, the task force finalized the purpose. It was decided that "I'd Sooner

Read" would be an initiative designed to:
- Promote the value of reading for individuals and families,
- Establish a positive image of Oklahoma as a reading state,
- Publicize and encourage participation in Oklahoma's existing reading incentive and literacy programs, and
- Encourage reading by Oklahomans of all ages.

Official participants of "I'd Sooner Read" are Oklahoma's public and private school library media centers, public libraries, and literacy programs. Evidence of participation will be the contribution of data on the numbers of books read by school and public library users. Library users may also report the reading done by family members or even friends and neighbors so that students are encouraged to talk about reading to their parents and adult friends and collect reading data from them.

Oklahoma's school and public libraries have been asked to help encourage their readers to count the books they have read and contribute those figures to help Oklahoma reach a reading goal of 12,647,608 books. Oklahoma's goal is the state's share of a billion, based upon population figures. Books read by anyone and everyone may be counted. Teachers and librarians may count the numbers collected for "The Principal's Challenge," the "Book-It" program, books read for the Accelerated Reader program, or other such incentive programs. The goal is not to create a separate count, but to collect reading data while adding a new dimension of excitement to reading. What counts as a book will be left to

the discretion of local librarians. Anything local school and public libraries accept and any way they choose to define a book is acceptable by this task force. Librarians have been encouraged to look for a way that students can record their own reading, they have also been encouraged to establish their own library's goal.

Timeline and Activities

The task force meets monthly. Originally, the task force established a two-year timeline with the conclusion of the project planned for Oklahoma's 90th birthday, November 1997. When AASL determined that the final count would be made in April 1997, the timeline was revised. Significant events for the project were:

June 1995	First meeting of the Task Force
September 1995	"I'd Sooner Read" introduced at the Encyclo-Media
November 1995	Official kickoff of "I'd Sooner Read"
February 1996	Publication of the first issue of the "I'd Sooner Read Guide"
March 1996	"I'd Sooner Read" buffalo begin to travel the state, accompanied by their scrapbooks
June 1996	Television commercials first aired
August 1996	Printing of "I'd Sooner Read" poster (Kim Doner, Illustrator)
September 1996	Publication of the second issue of the "I'd Sooner Read Participant's Guide"
September 1996	Program promoting "I'd Sooner Read" at Encyclo-Media and Posters distributed to school libraries at Encyclo-Media
September 1996	Monthly "count" news releases to state newspapers begins
November 1996	"Stampede to Read," major promotion effort
March 1997	Final count

Creating a Theme and Image

The "I'd Sooner Read" theme and a buffalo "mascot" grew from a desire to tailor the project specifically to Oklahoma. A wide focus that targets readers of all ages and a broad base of support also make Oklahoma's "I'd Sooner Read" project unique.

51

Oklahoma's Project Unique: I'd Sooner Read!

Introducing the Effort at "Encyclo-Media"

Sponsored by the Oklahoma State Department of Education and developed to support state school library development efforts, Encyclo-Media is an annual gathering, which has now broadened its focus to include instructional technology and gifted education. It draws more than 2,000 school and public librarians, teachers and administrators. In September 1995 the "I'd Sooner Read" program was held at Encyclo-Media to introduce the project and solicit input. A follow-up occurred in September 1996.

Participants' Guide Developed

Members of the task force contributed to a guide that was published in a newspaper format and mailed to all school and public libraries and literacy offices across the state. The *Daily Oklahoman* contributed the layout and printing of the first issue. The Oklahoma State Department of Education contributed the mailing to school libraries, and the Oklahoma Department of Libraries contributed the mailing to public libraries and literacy offices. The guide included bibliographies, a sample letter to parents, a history of the buffalo's return to Oklahoma in 1907, and a variety of ideas for counting books read and promoting reading. A second issue was distributed in September 1996 and focused on the "Stampede to Read" event held in November 1996.

Promotional Efforts

What could be more fun, we thought, than a visit from a stuffed buffalo? Buffalo created by a seamstress from a small Oklahoma town have become the symbol of the project. Several were sponsored by banks and other businesses to visit Oklahoma libraries. These buffalo travel with a scrapbook to record activities held in their honor. OETA, Oklahoma's public television station, contributed the development of commercials for "I'd Sooner Read." These have aired on OETA beginning in June 1996, and they are being distributed to commercial stations. A picture of the "I'd Sooner Read" poster and the sounds of a buffalo stampede accompany the narration.

Kim Doner, winner of the 1995 Oklahoma Center for the Book award for illustration, donated her talents to the creation of a poster to promote and celebrate "I'd Sooner Read." Her poster shows a father and child on the back of a buffalo bursting through the pages of a book.

In September 1995, the task force began to send information out through the Oklahoma Press Association. Participants were encouraged to send press releases to individual newspapers about local school and public library activities related to "I'd Sooner Read." They were also encouraged to communicate with their communities in other ways, for example, letters to parents of school children.

The "Stampede to Read," was developed to coincide with National Children's Book Week and Oklahoma's 89th birthday. Additional efforts that involve adults and children were also developed.

Creative Connections

The Kim Doner poster is an exciting outcome of "I'd Sooner Read." Another is the research into the history of the return of the buffalo to Oklahoma in 1907. This was completed by two of task force members. They researched and wrote an article for the first issue of the "I'd Sooner Read" participant's guide. This article may become a children's book. Watch for more information on this exciting development!

Conclusion and Suggestions

Experience suggests that creative committee members representing a broad base of interests are essential ingredients in a successful project. A great debt is owed to Oklahoma public library members who have been active contributors.

At last count, Oklahomans had read well over one million books. There is a long road ahead to reach the goal of twelve million, but some pretty unexpected things have already been accomplished; so, the goal may be reached "Sooner" than you'd expect!

Anne Masters is the director of Media Service and Instructional Technology for Norman Public Schools in Norman, Oklahoma. She is the chair of the Oklahoma Count on Reading Task Force.

53

I'd Sooner Read – Program Materials

54

What is I'D SOONER READ?

I'D SOONER READ is an Oklahoma reading initiative designed to
• promote the value of reading for individuals and families

OKLAHOMA
RUSHING
TO HELP
THE NATION
READ
1,000,000,000
BOOKS!

Who can participate in I'D SOONER READ?

Official participants of I'D SOONER READ will be Oklahoma's public and private school library media centers and public libraries. Evidence of participation will be the contribution of data on the numbers of books read by school and public library patrons.

What is Oklahoma's Goal?

Oklahoma's goal will announced in November. It will be our state's share of "A Billion Books" based upon population.

What happens when Oklahoma reaches its goal?

We will celebrate Oklahoma's 90th birthday in November of 1997 with a big event and the announcement of the number of books read.

Why should a school or public library participate and contribute reading data?

You will be contributing to the achievement of Oklahoma's reading goal as well as the national goal of a "Billion Books"; state reading data will be publicized regularly.

You will receive a certificate of participation from the Office of the Governor.

Celebrity visits will be made to participating public and school libraries. The libraries will be selected by drawing. The Governor and First Lady are expected to participate. Other celebrities are being contacted.

Watch for the Reading Buffalo who will begin travelling the state this November!

How will data be collected and contributed?

School and public libraries will determine their own methods for encouraging reading and for collecting data.

A method of reporting data to the state will be announced in November.

What information will participating school and public libraries receive?

Participating libraries will receive a PR Packet containing:
• Information explaining I'D SOONER READ.
• Information identifying organized state reading and adult literacy incentive, promotion, and assistance programs (with contact persons).
• Reporting procedures.
• Information about celebrity readers and the mysterious Reading Buffalo.

PART TWO

ACTIVITIES FROM AN ESTABLISHED READING INITIATIVE 55

Great Ideas from Indiana's REAP Project

Linda Cornwell

Editor's Introductory Note

No doubt about it, Hoosiers love to read. This is clearly evident in the enthusiastic reports supplied to the Indiana Department of Education's Office of Learning Resources by schools participating in the Reading Excitement and Paperbacks (REAP) project. Indiana's approach to developing life-long readers was already well established as AASL's Count on Reading project powered up, and thus a groundswell was underway for making connections to the national endeavor. For those looking for fresh ideas and activities to ignite the spark of reading, look no further! Indiana has ideas aplenty and if you need to spark or rekindle your own programs, you can borrow a page or two from Indiana's book of success stories.

As this book goes to press, the youngest Hoosiers have obviously made an impression on their elders — Indiana's Superintendent of Public Instruction, Dr. Suellen Reed, announced the 1997 Reading & Literacy Initiative for a Better Indiana. The proposal is the centerpiece of the Department of Education's legislative agenda for the upcoming session of Indiana's General Assembly.

"To increase student performance, to increase literacy, to promote a skilled work force, and to increase economic development, we must focus on enhancing the reading proficiency of Indiana students," said Reed.

The program will focus specifically on three areas: (1) early Intervention programs such as Reading Recovery for early grade levels; (2) a renewed investment in school library books; and (3) adequate funding for the state's adult education/literacy programs.

In regard to the second component of the initiative, School Library Books, Indiana recognizes that studies show that high scores on college entrance exams are closely correlated to the local per pupil dollars spent on library media centers. Currently, Indiana school districts purchase the equivalent of one-half book per student per year. The purchase of school library books has not kept pace with the demand. Assistance to elementary and middle schools to replenish inadequate print materials in their school libraries is a necessity. One source has cited that the average book in an Indiana school library has a copyright date of 1968. The initiative will provide a $1 for $1 match by the state to local school corporations for the purchase of library materials. The goal of this initiative is to help elementary and middle schools with a one-time grant for the purchase of two books per student per year of the biennium.

In Indiana, public input from a series of Town Meetings that the Department of Education conducted over several months showed that Reading Initiatives along with Essential Skills ranked highest among the public's priorities of education concerns. Dr. Reed was joined in her announcement by Indiana State Representatives Sue Scholer (R-West Lafayette), Sheila Klinker (D-Lafayette), and Cleo Duncan (R-Greensburg) — all coauthors of the bill and representatives of at least twenty-five education stakeholders and organizations offering their endorsements. The bill will be introduced in the House of Representatives by Rep. B. Patrick Bauer (D-South Bend).

After you review the variety of ways in which dedicated Indiana educators have fostered the love of reading in their students, it's no wonder that with the common sense that is the hallmark of the Midwest, Indiana is ready, willing and anxious to leverage this success and give their kids access to books, books and MORE books!

Background

To develop a love of reading, children need time to read, access to high interest reading materials, and teachers who encourage independent reading. Recognizing these key ingredients, the Indiana Department of Education through the Office of Learning Resources launched the Reading Excitement and Paperbacks (REAP) project to encourage young people to develop a lifelong interest in reading. The REAP project received funding from Lilly Endowment, Inc.

The REAP project provides grants to upper elementary and junior high schools in Indiana to establish recreational reading collections and to implement activities, integrating independent reading into the classroom.

Each participating school is responsible for designing its own program geared to the particular needs and interests of the children served. Activities include an array of events to incorporate independent reading into the school day and to promote reading at home, such as sleep-ins, cross-age level reading, read-a-thons, guest readers, theme weeks, turn off television campaigns, storytelling, battle of the books, lunch bunch reading clubs, book talks, reading fairs, student/parent reading teams.

Office of Learning Resources personnel working with the REAP project visit each site to provide guidance for teachers and parents in book sharing strategies, reading incentive techniques, parent involvement, and principles of book selection.

Linda Cornwell is the learning resources consultant for the Indiana Department of Education. She is the manager of Project REAP and Reading Educate Indiana Program Coordinator. She is the Count on Reading Committee Program co-chair there.

57

Great Ideas from Indiana's REAP Project

READING IS SHARING AT DURGAN ELEMENTARY SCHOOL

Durgan Elementary School • 1840 South 18th Street • Lafayette, IN • 47905 • 317-449-3650

Grace Gillespie, Site Coordinator

Durgan Elementary School discovered the meaning of its particular REAP theme: "Reading is Sharing." Through their years of participation in the REAP project, students, staff, community, and parents have demonstrated that they share the joy of reading.

Durgan students have grown up with the REAP project and have had many opportunities to share reading. Two of Durgan's many programs are Reading Circles and ARROW.

Modeling — A Key Ingredient

Children have learned via their experiences at Durgan, that reading is a way of life. They have seen their teachers model reading as a fun, enjoyable experience. A staff reading circle was started as a result of the REAP project. The students see staff members reading a selection of the month during Sustained Quiet Uninterrupted Individual Reading Time (SQUIRT), discussing the selection with one another throughout the month, and wearing their "Reading is Sharing" sweatshirt on the day that the reading circle meets.

Arrows Really Read on Weekends (ARROW) has given parents and students a fun way to share reading activities during one weekend a month. The goals of this particular program were to promote literacy, portray reading as a fun activity and an enjoyable part of family life, and involve families in the students' learning.

The students took home tic-tac-toe sheets filled with reading experiences — geared for that particular month — to "share" with a parent. The activities covered a wide range of ideas, including reading all kinds of materials together, going to festivals and concerts, doing holiday-related activities, and playing games. Participants chose which activities they wanted to complete and filled out the sheet. Any tic-tac-toe (three in a row completed), returned by a predetermined deadline with a parent signature, qualified them for a drawing where the winners received tickets for parent and child to attend various local events. Teachers in the fourth and fifth grades shared the responsibility with the media specialist for gathering and distributing donated prizes and for making the game boards.

Results

This program not only encouraged students and their families to make an effort to do reading and family activities together, but also gave winning students and their families opportunities to attend local art, music, and sporting events.

The entire REAP project has been a wonderful experience for the whole Durgan community. Sharing reading experiences has given students self-respect, reading skills, and an enjoyable activity that they can continue to share with one another throughout their lives.

58

Great Ideas from Indiana's REAP Project

SOUTH SIDE'S READ 'N FEED

South Side Middle School • 101 West 29th Street • Anderson, IN • 46016 • 317-641-2051

Vickie Thomas and Karen Sipes, Site Coordinators

Project Overview

Offering students and facilitators a unique book discussion experience, the Read N' Feed program at South Side Middle School was held once a month, with participants taking part in a forty-minute discussion on a novel over lunch. This reading enrichment experience was offered to any student who volunteered to read a selected novel in three weeks and then join with other students at lunchtime to "feed" and participate in a small-group discussion of the title.

Read 'N Feed gave students the opportunity to share their feelings and ideas about what they read in a nonthreatening, nongraded environment. The program's goal was to change student attitudes about reading — to help them see reading as an enjoyable, lifelong activity.

Meals for the program were provided by various local fast-food restaurants, and faculty and/or guests from the community facilitated the group activities. Many of the guest's experiences and occupations related to the novels discussed (e.g. Vietnam veterans, lawyers, the superintendent, and the girl wrestlers among others).

The program, which appealed to all ability levels within the student population, incorporated cooperative learning strategies, utilized community resource guests, and embraced risk-taking.

A committee of three teachers, the library media specialist, and the young adult librarian from the local public library, selected seven young adult novels each year for the program that targeted seventh and eighth graders. Consideration was given to a variety of genres, as well as to an equal number of male and female main characters.

Planning

Planning for the program began in August with the selection of titles and the scheduling of Read 'N Feed dates (September, November, January, and April). Each session took about a month to organize, and weekly committee planning meetings were necessary to brainstorm, share ideas, make programming decisions, design the discussion outline, and assign responsibilities.

Resources

Resources needed were about seventy-five copies of each novel, supplies, or decorations, companion novels, picture books, media, guest readers, and of course discussion participants. The resources varied with each novel, depending on content.

Personnel and Follow-up Activities

Support personnel included the members of the Reading Motivation Committee, faculty who helped facilitate group discussions, and parent volunteers.

Follow-up activities such as creating murals, writing to authors, writing letters to the editor, and watching related videos served to extend the learning experiences of the novel discussions.

59

Great Ideas from Indiana's REAP Project

QUICK READS AT NORTHSIDE

Northside Middle School • 1400 27th Street • Columbus, IN • 47210 • 812-376-4403

Carol Helton and Nancy Nyers, Site Coordinators

Rewarding Teachers Who Read

Quick Reads, one of the most successful of many activities employed as part of the REAP project at Northside, involved all teachers and students in the reading process by rewarding teachers for reading to students during the advisee period at the end of the school day.

Encouraging Teacher Participation

"Quick Reads" began with a REAP kick-off at the faculty meeting in September. The staff was treated to a celebration with cake and punch, and a prize was awarded to one faculty member who read a short selection to illustrate that teachers can enjoy reading aloud.

At the next faculty meeting, a gift certificate was given to a teacher who volunteered to read. Involving members of the staff in reading to each other set the stage for the next step of the program.

Program Details

Each teacher was given a set of entry forms, and days were set aside for a "Teacher Read-a-Rama." During a two-week period, each teacher who read to his or her advisee students submitted an entry form recording each five-minute period that the reading took place. These forms had to be validated by signatures of two students. Teachers received double points for reading done by guests (as long as no more than three guests read within that two-week period).

At the end of each week, a drawing of the entries determined which classes would win parties. Naturally, the class with the most entries had the best chance of winning the draw. In addition, the total number of minutes read by each teacher was tabulated, and the teacher who had read the most won a dinner certificate for two at a quality restaurant.

After that, teachers were encouraged to read to their students for five to fifteen minutes a day. At the end of the grading period, teachers submitted a tally of their "quick reads," and the teacher who had read the most number of minutes received a gift certificate.

There is abundant evidence establishing that kids like to be read to and that this activity should not be curtailed as they mature into adolescence. Northside's innovative approach to reward their teachers for creating and modeling a daily reading habit no doubt helped to foster greater value among students for the activity, as well as helped establish a closer sense of community within the school.

Great Ideas from Indiana's REAP Project

LITERARY LUNCH AT THE McCULLOCH MIDDLE SCHOOL

McCulloch Middle School • 3528 South Washington Street • Marion, IN • 46953 • 317-674-6917

Artis Ann Hoffmann and Virginia Lake, Site Coordinators

The Program

Literary Lunch, held once every six-week grading period, was one of the motivational strategies used at the McCulloch Middle School to promote reading by sixth graders. Students who had done well on class book reports, met in the school library for lunch. A relaxed atmosphere was created by using table cloths and candles. After lunch, students discussed books and presented skits or poems.

Pre-Planning and Resources

Preplanning included creation and distribution of blank book report sandwiches, scheduling the library, set up of lunch tables, and buying treats. The activity was coordinated by the school librarian and a different language arts teacher every six weeks. Resources (cost approximately $10 per luncheon) included colored paper, dessert-type treats, candles, tablecloths, paperbacks and *Mailbox* magazine.

Each lunch held during the year involved students from a different one of the six language arts groups in the school. The "price of admission" was a book report sandwich created by the students to compliment the theme "We're Hungry for Good Books! Mmmmm-Good!" At each Literary Lunch, a free paperback was given away for the best-written book report sandwich. These were later displayed near the library.

Great Ideas from Indiana's REAP Project

DEXTER SCHOOL "PIGS OUT" ON BOOKS!

Dexter Elementary School • 917 South Dexter Avenue • Evansville, IN • 47714 • 812-476-1321

Karen Kuester, Site Coordinator

Promoting Reading for Enjoyment

To foster family reading activities and to promote reading for enjoyment, students and their families read together for the equivalent of fifteen to twenty minutes per day. This activity time could include reading silently or reading aloud. Weekly reading record sheets, signed by parents and returned to school, earned points toward receiving an invitation to the "Great Pig Out Party" and chances in a weekly drawing.

Project Particulars

Students earned points towards the Pig Out Party by completing activities such as visiting the public library, bringing in a photo of their family reading together, making a mobile depicting scenes from a book, making a life-size model or picture of a book character or object, writing book reviews, writing and mailing a letter to the author or illustrator of a favorite book, or rewriting a story with a new ending, setting or characters. Students also had the option of creating their own activities such as demonstrating a magic trick, or telling jokes from a joke book. Parents were encouraged to assist students with their projects.

Students were chosen, through weekly drawings, to have lunch at the Braves' Club Cafe (media center) with a celebrity guest. Guests included a college basketball coach, the mayor, a local weatherman, a TV news reporter and the principal. Guests at each luncheon were served favorite foods from local restaurants. Students also received a souvenir that related to the celebrity guests, such as a pompom for the basketball coach.

Drawings were also held each week for free books. Students earning a designated number of points by the end of the program earned the privilege of attending the Pig Out Party, which included "Make Your Own Sundaes" and a magician who linked his presentation to the magic of reading.

Well Worth the Cost

The cost of the eight-week program was $250. Most of the food was donated. Positive responses included great responses from students, parents, and staff and increased book circulation.

Great Ideas from Indiana's REAP Project

LEW WALLACE STUDENTS BOARD THE READING SUCCESS EXPRESS

Lew Wallace Elementary • 6235 Jefferson Avenue • Hammond, IN • 46234 • 219-933-2479
Judy Marzocchi, Site Coordinator

Background

The Lew Wallace REAP theme was Get on Board the Success Express and Travel! Students applied for a passport to travel on the Success Express (the school's motto). The students could travel to anywhere in the world by completing an individualized reading contract. Staff members were able to make a number of curriculum connections in relation to the theme and to integrate an even greater variety of instructional strategies.

Program in Action

The designated REAP area was decorated with many travel posters of countries from all across the globe. Large throw pillows, chairs and stools, were on hand in the area so that students could relax and read. This area was strictly for free-time pleasure reading. The fourth and fifth grade students were often spotted selecting just the right pillow for nestling up with just the right book.

All fourth- and fifth-grade students created their own passports. These in turn were kept in a REAP folder developed expressly for their portfolios. Government Officials (the teachers and school library media personnel), explained how important passports are when you travel outside of the U.S.A. They obviously made their point, and there were no lost or misplaced passports throughout the entire year!

63

Reading Contracts

The Students entered into monthly reading contract agreements with their classroom teacher, parents, and Title One teacher stating the number of books to be read each month. All parties involved had to sign the document in order for it to be "official." This helped to ensure that, with appropriate adult guidance, the number of books to be read correlated to student reading ability. Once the contract was "signed, sealed, and delivered," students were "on board" the Reading Express.

The government officials made regular "stops" in the classroom and students presented their passports for the required stamps to complete their particular reading journey. Stops were scheduled on "even" and "odd" days and signaled what the student should expect as an incentive to continue the trip. Even-numbered stops meant that the media specialist would appear with a treasure chest containing envelopes that held slips of paper indicating what prize was won. Items included free homework passes, t-shirts, lunch with the principal, pencils, key chains, and extra reading time to name but a few. On odd-numbered stop days, students who fulfilled their contract terms could expect the opportunity to select a paperback book to add to his or her home library.

Continued on next page

Great Ideas from Indiana's REAP Project

The kids especially loved the draw of the Treasure Chest and greeted the media specialist with great enthusiasm.

In addition to the Reading Express, Lew Wallace students were also invited to participate in helping to select books that they wanted to see added to their REAP collection. This brought an increased sense of ownership and pride.

Unexpected Benefits

This program was constructed on the idea that students, who have access to a print-rich environment and who participate in the selection of the materials available, will read more and will read better. Evidence suggested by the high rate of contract completion and the documentation of improved reading scores shows this is true. Staff members were delighted to hear students talking book plots with one another as well as bringing books with them to lunch and recess, and they were overjoyed when a particularly reluctant reader signed his first contract.

Lew Wallace students, teachers, and parents are sold on the Reading Express and on REAP. A reading spark has started to glow and needs to continue to be fueled in order to keep it bright so that kids become life-long readers.

64

PROMOTING INDEPENDENT READING
A CHECKLIST FOR SCHOOL LIBRARY MEDIA CENTERS

		Yes	No
1.	Are all students allowed flexible access to the school library media center throughout the school day?		
2.	Is the school library media center staffed by a full-time, certified school library media specialist?		
3.	Is the school library media center staff knowledgeable about children's literature?		
4.	Does the school library media center staff routinely recommend books or other materials to students and staff to read?		
5.	Does the school library media center staff promote books and reading through booktalks, book displays, book fairs, and reading motivation/incentive programs?		
6.	Does the school library media center have a large collection of appealing, high-interest, relevant reading materials that students enjoy reading?		
7.	Does the school library media center spend the equivalent of two books per student per year on books and other reading materials?		
8.	Does the school library media center's circulation policy permit each student to check out an unlimited number of reading materials?		
9.	Does the school library media center provide classroom collections for independent reading?		

65

Great Ideas from Indiana's REAP Project

		Yes	No
10.	Does the school library media center staff provide teacher in-service related to new books, reading strategies, and reading motivation techniques?	_____	_____
11.	Does the school library media center staff model enthusiasm for reading?	_____	_____
12.	Does the school library media center staff actively cooperate with the public library to promote reading?	_____	_____
13.	Does the school library media center staff plan and/or implement projects in cooperation with teachers to promote reading?	_____	_____
14.	Does the school library media center staff solicit the assistance of teachers and students in updating the center's collection of reading materials?	_____	_____
15.	Does the school climate convey the message that reading is a highly valued activity and a priority within the school?	_____	_____
16.	Is there a school-wide sustained silent reading program in place?	_____	_____
17.	Is every student read aloud to every day for a minimum of fifteen minutes by at least one teacher?	_____	_____
18.	Are parents encouraged to be involved in the reading motivation/incentive program?	_____	_____

Total Score _____ _____

Yes Quotient
18-16 Great
15-14 Good
13-below Needs Work

Linda Cornwell
Indiana Department of
Education

Program Materials

RECOMMENDED READINGS ON READING
A SELECTED ANNOTATED BIBLIOGRAPHY
JANUARY 1997

Birkerts, Sven. *The Gutenberg Elegies: The Fate of Reading in an Electronic Age.*
Boston: Faber and Faber, 1994. ISBN 0-571-19849-X

Birkerts explores the impact of emerging technologies on the printed page and the
reader-writer exchange while maintaining that literature offers a wisdom that cannot
be found in either electronic communications or information processing
technologies.

Bushman, John H. & Bushman, Kay P. *Using Young Adult Literature in the English
Classroom.* New York: Macmillan Publishing, 1993. ISBN 0-02-317532-X

The authors argue that contemporary young adult literature deserves the same
attention and respect that is currently given the classics in middle and high school
English classes and that young adult literature should be used in the classroom as a
bridge to adult literature.

Carlsen, Robert G. & Sherrill, A. *Voices of Readers: How We Come to Love Books.*
Urbana, IL: National Council of Teachers of English, 1988. ISBN 0-8141-
5639-8

In an attempt to answer the question, "How does a person come to acquire a love
for literature (and reading)?" the authors chronicle the literacy histories of both
readers and non-readers.

Chambers, Aidan. *The Reading Environment: How Adults Help Children Enjoy
Books.* New York: Stenhouse, 1996. ISBN 1-57110-029-6

Chambers provides a rationale for independent reading and offers practical advice
and comment on how schools can help children become thoughtful, willing readers.

Cramer, Eugene & Castle, Harrietta, eds. *Fostering the Love of Reading: The
Affective Domain in Reading Education.* Newark, DE: International Reading
Association, 1994. ISBN 0-87207-125-1

67

The editors present a collection of articles that focus on reading motivation and the role that teachers play in helping children develop into engaged readers who read both for pleasure and information.

Drutman, Ava & Houston, D. *150 Surefire Ways to Keep Them Reading All Year!* New York: Scholastic Professional Books, 1991. ISBN 0-590-49142-3

This text is a compendium of ideas and activities for elementary teachers. Chapters include "Places and Spaces for Books;" "Awareness of Books and Their Special Parts;" "Authors and Illustrators;" "Celebrations, Awards, Games;" "Special Days and Seasons;" "Response."

Krashen, Stephen. *The Power of Reading: Insight from the Research.* Englewood, CO: Libraries Unlimited, Inc., 1993. ISBN 1-56308-006-0

This is a small, very readable, and powerfully packed book of the author's research, conclusions, and recommendations about the literacy crisis. "Nearly everyone in the U. S. can read and write... Although [they] clearly don't read and write well enough to handle complex literacy demands of modern society. The cure... lies... in doing one activity... that is all too often rare in the lives of many people: reading."

Leonhardt, Mary. *Parents Who Love Reading, Kids Who Don't: How It Happens and What You Can Do About It.* New York: Crown Publishers, 1993. ISBN 0-517-59164-2

Although this book is directed at parents, it is equally or more important for teachers. Leonhardt outlines what parents and teachers can do to kindle or rekindle the joy of reading in reluctant readers.

Manquel, Alberto. *A History of Reading.* New York: Viking, 1996. ISBN 0-670-84302-4

In a series of eloquent essays, Manquel presents the history of reading, shares his discoveries about the reading habit, and celebrates his conviction that the "history of reading has no end."

Monseau, Virginia & Salvner, Gary, eds. *Reading Their World: The Young Adult Novel in the Classroom.* Portsmouth, NH: Heinemann, 1992. ISBN 0-86709-306-4

Program Materials

This book, of interest to secondary teachers, examines the issues related to young adult literature, how to make a literature class into a community of readers, and how to integrate young adult novels into the traditional literature curriculum.

Monseau, Virginia. *Responding to Young Adult Literature*. Portsmouth, NH: Heinemann, 1996. ISBN 0-86709-401-X

Monseau shows secondary English teachers what can happen when students are given the opportunity to read young adult literature and how a response approach to young adult literature can work in the classroom.

Nell, Victor. *Lost in a Book: The Psychology of Reading for Pleasure*. New Haven: Yale University Press, 1988. ISBN 0-300-04906-4

Intriguing insights into the process of reading for pleasure are presented: why people read; its similarity to hypnosis and dreaming; why sophisticated readers often enjoy "trash." A comprehensive and scholarly study, it is thorough, well-written, and filled with the joy of reading.

Pelton, Mary Helen. *Reading is Not a Spectator Sport*. Englewood, CO: Teacher Ideas Press, 1993. ISBN 1-56308-118-0

The author presents hundreds of ideas to encourage students to love and respond to literature. Reading incentive programs, cooperative learning and literature, thematic units are just a few of the topics covered.

Pennac, Daniel. *Better Than Life*. Toronto: Coach House Press, 1994. ISBN 0-88910-484-0

Pennac shares his love of reading and relates ways to restore that love to disenchanted young adult readers.

Reed, Arthea. *Comics to Classics: A Parent's Guide to Books for Teens and Pre-teens*. Newark, DE: International Reading Association, 1988. ISBN 0-87207-798-5

This is a good discussion of adolescent reading - their needs and interests, family reading, book selection, and the giving and borrowing of books. An annotated bibliography of "books that kids love" is also included.

Great Ideas from Indiana's REAP Project

Rosenthal, Nadine. *Speaking of Reading.* Portsmouth, NH: Heinemann, 1995. ISBN 0-435-08199-5

Through oral histories of diverse readers, Rosenthal, provides insight into reading and the reading process while focusing attention on the crucial role of reading in our lives.

Schell, Leo. *How to Create an Independent Reading Program.* New York: Scholastic Books, 1991. ISBN 0-590-49135-0

This text provides teacher-tested, practical ideas for getting elementary students involved in a year long independent read program. Tips on creating an environment conducive to reading, building and sustaining an independent reading program, establishing a school library media center connection, and more are valuable inclusions.

Spiegel, Dixie Lee. *Reading for Pleasure: Guidelines.* Newark, DE: International Reading Association, 1981. ISBN 0-87207-226-6

This readable, how-to book explains in-depth how to develop, initiate, and manage a dynamic independent reading program in the classroom.

Linda Cornwell
Indiana Department of Education

Program Materials

SELECTED BOOK REVIEW

ANNUAL LISTS

The American Library Association
50 East Huron Street
Chicago, Illinois

- *Best Books for Young Adults* (YALSA)
- *Editor's Choice* (*Booklist*)
- *Notable Books* (RUSA)
- *Notable Children's Books* (ALSC)
- *Peace and Understanding through Children's Books* (ALSC)
- *Popular Paperbacks for Young Adults* (YALSA)
- *Outstanding Books for the College Bound* (YALSA)
- *Quick Picks for Reluctant Young Adult Readers* (YALSA)

Children's Book Council
350 Scotland Road
Orange, New Jersey 07050

- *Notable Children's Trade Books in the Field of Social Studies*
- *Outstanding Science Trade Books for Children*

Cooperative Children's Books
Post Office Box 5288
Madison, Wisconsin 53705

- *CCBC Choices*

International Reading Association
800 Barksdale Road
Post Office Box 8139
Newark, Delaware 19714

- *Children's Choices*
- *Young Adult's Choices*
- *Teacher's Choices*

PERIODICALS

The ALAN Review (Gr. 7-12)
Assembly on Literature for Adolescents
National Council of Teachers of English
1111 Kenyon Boulevard
Urbana, Illinois 61801

71

Great Ideas from Indiana's REAP Project

Booklist (Gr. K-12)
American Library Association
50 East Huron Street
Chicago, Illinois 60611

Book Links (Gr. K-8)
American Library Association
50 East Huron Street
Chicago, Illinois 60611

Bulletin of the Center for Children's Books (Gr. K-12)
University of Illinois
1325 South Oak
Champaign, Illinois 61820

Children's Book Reviews (Gr. K-12)
Children's Book Review Magazine
Post Office Box 5082
Brentwood, Tennessee 37024-5082
(800)543-7220 (subscriptions)

Horn Book (Gr. K-12)
Kirkus Services, Incorporated
200 Park Avenue South
New York, New York 10003

Kliatt Paperback Book Guide (Gr. 7-12)
425 Watertown Street
Newton, Massachusetts 02158

The New Advocate (Gr. K-8)
Christopher-Gordon Publishers
480 Washington Street
Norwood, Massachusetts 02062

New York Times Book Review (Gr. K-12)
New York Times Company
229 West 43rd Street
New York, New York 10036

School Library Journal (Gr. K-12)
Bowker Magazine Group
Cahner's Magazine Division
249 West 17th Street
New York, New York 10011

Program Materials

Voices of Youth Advocates (Gr. 7-12)
Scarecrow Press
Post Office Box 4167
Metuchen, New Jersey 08840

The Web (Gr. K-8)
Ohio State University
College of Education
Columbus, Ohio 43210

BOOKS

Adventuring with Books: A Booklist for Pre-K-Grade 6
Books for You: A Booklist for Senior High Students
High Interest, Easy Reading: A Booklist for Junior and Senior High School Students
Your Reading: A Booklist for Junior High and Middle School Students
National Council of Teachers of English
1111 Kenyon Boulevard
Urbana, Illinois 61801

Best Books for Children: Preschool Through Grade 6
Best Books for Junior High Readers
Best Books for Senior High Readers
R. R. Bowker Company
121 Chanlon Road
New Providence, New Jersey 07974

73

Linda Cornwell
Indiana Department of Education

PART THREE

WHAT RESEARCH TELLS US

TIPS FOR PLANNING READING MOTIVATION PROGRAMS

The Krashen Connection: *The Power of Reading*

*T*he lessons of Stephen Krashen's compelling work, The Power of Reading, *resound throughout the* Count on Reading Handbook. *Time and again, the research reviewed by Krashen, and the evidence it cites to provide opportunities for young people to become independent readers, is reiterated by our authors as indicators of their own successes.*

While it is important for reading initiatives to occur in order to foster the love of reading, it is more important to examine the proof of their connections to academic achievement. To improve the current condition of reading in our country (where only 25 percent of fourth graders, 28 percent of eighth graders, and 34 percent of twelfth graders reached the "proficient" level of reading according to the 1994 National Assessment of Educational Progress report) efforts must continue to help Americans understand that reading is an

acquired skill — the more students read, the better they read. Educators must become fluent in citing the research and in developing clear associations between the availability and accessibility of print-rich environments and reading-role models to the development of positive reading habits, reading enjoyment and improved academic achievement.

What follows is a summary of Krashen's analysis of the research of one hundred years in the field of reading. These are the results that initiatives like Count on Reading hope to duplicate, and they form the basis for putting reading promotion into educational context. In addition, presented in this text are the results of one of Krashen's latest efforts in examining the relationship between school and public libraries and the National Assessment of Educational Progress Reading Scores.

The Power of Reading: A Research Perspective

Kimberly Taylor

from Colorado's Read the Rockies Participant's Package

Stephen Krashen is the author of The Power of Reading (*Libraries Unlimited*, 1993), *a review of one hundred years of reading research. Through examining this extensive research, he has concluded that reading is the most powerful tool available for building vocabulary and increasing the ability to read, write, spell, and comprehend. He specifically discusses the value of reading aloud, light reading, and reading nontraditional forms of literature, as well as the importance of the library and a print-rich environment. He advocates a program of free voluntary reading in the schools. Regular, sustained reading promotions like National Library Week and Summer Reading lend support to the concept of free voluntary reading. Some of Krashen's conclusions follow:*

- In thirty-eight of forty-one studies, students using free voluntary reading (FVR) did as well or better in reading comprehension tests than students given traditional skill-based reading instruction.

- Reading as a leisure activity is the best predictor of comprehension, vocabulary, and reading speed.

- Two studies report higher scores on standardized tests when FVR was used.

- The relationship between reported FVR and literacy is remarkably consistent.

- If children read one million words in a year, at least one thousand words will be added to their vocabulary.

- FVR is nearly always superior to direct instruction on tests of reading comprehension, vocabulary, writing, and grammar.

- Studies show that reading may be the only way to develop literacy skills.

- Hearing stories has a direct impact on literacy development.

- Children read more when they see other people reading.

- Light reading is how many people learn to read.

- Comic books are linguistically appropriate, not detrimental to reading development, and conduits to book reading.

School Libraries, Public Libraries, and the NAEP Reading Scores

Stephen D. Krashen

Reprinted with permission from *School Library Media Quarterly*, 23, no.4 (Summer 1995): 235–37

A multiple-regression analysis utilizing data from forty-one states was performed. Significant predictors of NAEP reading comprehension test scores were the number of books per student in school library media centers and average circulation in public libraries. The amount of software in school libraries was positively associated with reading scores, but not significantly. Surprisingly, increased library services was associated with lower reading scores.

The relationship between free reading and reading ability has been demonstrated in a wide variety of studies. Free reading, however, requires access to books; thus, it is no surprise to find positive correlation between access to books and reading ability.[1]

Children get a substantial percentage of books from libraries, both school and public, and some recent studies confirm that the quality of the library collection is a predictor of reading ability, both at the state level[2] and across countries.[3]

In this paper, the relationship between reading ability and library quality and use is probed for a single country, the United States, using states as a unit of analysis. In addition, because of the increasing investment by school libraries in computers and software,[4] the impact of software in school library media centers on reading is also investigated. Finally, it was of interest to determine whether those states that provided more school library services reported better reading scores.

Method

Fourth-grade scores on the 1992 NAEP Reading Comprehensive test were used as a measure of reading comprehension.[5] Scores from forty-one states were utilized, those for which complete data on other variables were available.

Data on elementary school library media centers were taken from White,[6] including the average number of books per student per state, the amount of software available ("machine-readable titles held"), and a measure of library service, which included the extent to which school library media centers provided services such as library skills instruction for students, inservices, reference assistance and technical assistance for teachers, and

interlibrary loans. Service scores were calculated by listing twenty-two possible services a library could provide and scoring each 0 (never performed), 1 (occasionally performed), or 2 (routinely performed).

No data on children's use of public libraries were found; Chute,[7] however, reported data on average circulation per capita. This figure could represent a general interest in reading among the state's residents, the quality of the state's libraries, and, at least to some extent, children's use of the library.

To control the effect of financial resources, expenditures per pupil for each of the forty-one states (1989–1990) were included in the analysis.[8]

Table 1
Descriptive Statistics

Variable	Mean	Standard Deviation
RC: NAEP score	216.51	8.52
SL: Books	17.146	5.12
SL: Software	29.780	18.89
SL: Service	22.780	3.04
PL	5.839	1.89
Exp	4903.01	1476.50

RC = scores on NAEP Reading Comprehension Test, fourth-graders.
SL: Books = school library: number of books per child; SL: Software = school library: software available; SL: Service = school library: services available; PL = public library, annual circulation per capita; Exp = expenditure per child.

Results

Table 1 presents descriptive statistics and table 2 presents intercorrelations for all variables. Reading comprehension scores are positively correlated with the number of books per students in school library media centers (p < .01)[9] as well as with library use (p < .01). A modest positive correlation was found between software in school library media centers and reading (p < .05), and, surprisingly, a clear negative correlation was found between reading ability and library services (p < .01).

Table 3 presents the results of a multiple-regression analysis in which all predictors were entered simultaneously. The results are similar to the correlational data in table 2: both public library and school library variables are significant predictors of reading scores, while library services is a strong negative predictor. The effect of software was positive but fell short of statistical significance, while expenditures per student had no effect. The predictors accounted for a remarkable 60 percent of the variance among reading scores.

Continued on next page

79

School Libraries, Public Libraries, and the NAEP Reading Scores

Discussion

Indicators of school library quality and public library use were significant predictors of reading comprehension scores. This supports, on a national level, previous findings at the state and international level, and is consistent with the many previous studies showing that free reading is a consistent predictor of reading ability and that libraries are a major source of reading for children.

The effect of software was positive and approached significance in the regression analysis. We have, however, no information about how the software was used, or whether it was used at all. In addition, Lance et al.[10] reported no impact of a school library computer factor (number of computers in the school library, number of instructional uses of computers) on reading comprehension scores for five of six grades investigated,[1,4,5,7,10] and found a negative relationship between the computing factor and reading scores for second-graders.

Expenditures for education did not affect reading comprehension test scores. Lance et al. also found that total school expenditures were not related to reading scores, but did report that money invested in the school library media center has an effect on collection size, which in turn affects reading test scores.[11] This suggests that for money to affect reading scores, it needs to be invested in the library.

The negative impact of library services is puzzling. It could mean that librarians who provide more services neglect more important aspects of the library: access to books. The negative relationship, however, could simply be a reflection of concern—librarians in states with low reading scores and less access to books may attempt to compensate by providing more services. This negative relationship, however, has not been reported elsewhere. Lance et al. reported that a factor labeled

Table 2
Intercorrelations among Variables

	SL: Books	SL: Software	SL: Service	PL	Exp
RC	.495[a]	.377[b]	-.513[a]	.559[a]	.058
SL: Books		.423[a]	-.035	.453[a]	.205
SL: Software			.041	.315[b]	.044
SL: Service				-.188	.051
PL					.090

$N = 41$; [a] $p < .01$; [b] $p < .05$

Library Media Specialist Role (hours per week for "media-endorsed staff hours and hours spent by…staff identifying materials for teacher-planned instructional units and collaborating with teachers in planning such units" [p. 60]), while not directly related to reading comprehension test scores, was related to the size of the library collection, which in turn was related to reading scores.[12]

The results of this study are thus not consistent with previous research in the areas of software and library services. They are, nonetheless, very consistent with research on reading and on the role of libraries, and provide indirect support for the hypothesis that it is reading that is largely responsible for literacy development.

Some caution is called for. The presence of some multi-collinearity,[13] as well as the fact that only one measure for each of the variables was used, indicates that replication is in order. The fact that the findings on the effects of the library are so similar to those reported in other studies, however, gives them some credibility.

Table 3
Multiple-Regression Analysis

Predictor	b	beta	stand.error	t	p
SL: Books	.4459	.2680	.2151	2.07	.046
SL: Software	.08659	.1929	.05403	1.59	.120
SL: Service	-1.2819	-.4566	.3073	-4.17	.0000
PL	1.3196	.2928	.5576	2.37	.024
Exp	-.000046	.0264	.0006309	-.07	.942

dependent variable = score on NAEP RC test
$r^2 = .062$; adjusted $r^2 = .545$; s = 5.746; F = 10.59: p < .001

Continued on next page

School Libraries, Public Libraries, and the NAEP Reading Scores

Acknowledgment

I thank Barry Gribbons and Daniel Krashen for helpful comments and suggestions on an earlier draft of this paper.

References and Notes

1. Stephen Krashen, *The Power of Reading* (Englewood, Colo.: Libraries Unlimited, 1993).

2. Keith Lance, Lynda Wellborn, and Christine Hamilton-Pennell, *The Impact of School Library Media Centers on Academic Achievement* (Castle Rock, Colo.: Hi Willow, 1993).

3. Warwick Elley, *How in the World Do Students Read?* (Hamburg, Germany: International Assn. of the Evaluation of Educational Achievement, 1992).

4. Marilyn Miller and Marilyn Shontz, "Expenditures for Resources in School Library Media Centers, FY 1991–92," *School Library Journal* 39 (Oct. 1993): 26-36.

5. Ina Mullis, Jay Campbell, and Alan Farstrup, *NAEP 1992 Reading Report Card for the Nation and the States.* Washington, D.C.: U.S. Dept. of Education, Office of Educational Research and Improvement, 1993.

6. Howard D. White, "School Library Collections and Services: Ranking the States," *SLMQ* 19 (Fall 1990): 13-26.

7. Adrienne Chute, *Public Libraries in the U.S.: 1990.* Washington, D.C.: U.S. Dept. of Education, Office of Educational Research and Improvement.

8. Mullis, Campbell, and Farstrup, *NAEP 1992 Reading Report Card.*

9. Inspection of the scatterplot for the correlation between books per student in school library media centers and reading scores revealed a hyperbolic relationship: high reading scores were possible with few books per student, but many books per student was consistently associated with a high reading score, suggesting that a good library will nearly always help, but that children may get books from other sources. A more linear relationship was found between the two variables by transforming the independent variable. Transforming x (books per student) into $-1/x$, for example, results in a correlation of .562, a modest improvement over the original .495. The original untransformed value was kept in the regression analysis for ease of interpretation.

10. Lance, Wellborn, and Hamilton-Pennell, *The Impact of School Library Centers on Academic Achievement.*

11. Ibid.

12. Ibid.

13. Because of the correlations among some of the predictors (table 2), a test of multicollinearity was performed; all independent variables were regressed on one another. The results confirmed the presence of some multicollinearity:

    dep. variable = r^2.
    SL: books = .643
    SL: software = .418
    SL: service = .052
    PL = .261
    exp = .043

    This modest degree of multicollinearity could be reduced by eliminating some predictors and doing a new analysis. Barry and Feldman (1985) note, however, that the consequences of misspecification are more serious than the consequences of multicollinearity. Thus, a new analysis was not performed. Instead, as Barry and Feldman suggest, we "recognize its presence but live with its consequences" (p. 49). The consequences include the fact that parameter estimates may vary widely among samples. Thus, replication of these results with other samples is called for (William Barry and Stanley Feldman, *Multiple Regression in Practice*). (Newbury Park, Calif.: Sage, 1985).

83

Susan D. Ballard is the director of Library, Media and Technology Services for the Londonderry School District in Londonderry, New Hampshire. She is co-chair of the New Hampshire Count on Reading State Steering Committee and a member of the AASL Count on Reading Task Force.